At the Going Down of the Sun

This book is dedicated to the memory
of my Father

George Edgar Boorman

who, together with both my Grandfathers,
served in the First World War
and fought in the Queen's Regiment
at Ypres, Loos and the Somme.

At the Going Down of the Sun

of the Sun

British First World War Memorials

Derek Boorman

*"They shall grow not old, as we that are
left grow old:
Age shall not weary them, nor the years condemn.
At the going down of the sun and in the morning
We will remember them"*

Laurence Binyon

William Sessions Limited
The Ebor Press
York, England

First Published October 1988

Copyright: Derek Boorman © 1988

ISBN 1 85072 041 X   Hardback

Printed in 10/11 point Bembo Typeface
by William Sessions Limited,
The Ebor Press, York, England.

CONTENTS

Except where otherwise stated, recent photographs
were taken by the Author.

The Streatham Memorial

Introduction

The First World War, or the Great War as it was known for so long, ended with the Armistice of 11th November, 1918. At the eleventh hour of the eleventh day of the eleventh month, fighting ceased, and the nations involved were able to consider the effect of the four years of brutal conflict.

In all, there were some 10 million dead and almost 30 million missing or wounded, wounded in many cases meaning maimed for life or blinded. Britain and the Empire alone had a million dead, and in one terrible day, the first day of the battle of the Somme, suffered 60,000 casualties of whom more than 20,000 were killed. Most of these casualties would have been within half-an-hour of the initial attack.

Five million men from the British Isles fought in the war, and each man had something like a one in three chance of being wounded, or a one in seven chance of never returning.

Nowadays, we can only wonder at the courage, discipline and loyalty of the men who fought in such a war. Between doomed attacks upon strongly held positions defended by machine guns, the front line soldier lived amidst mud and slime, surrounded by the bodies of friend and enemy alike, under constant threat of bombardment or sniping, and infested with lice.

In this year of the 70th anniversary of the Armistice, the youngest of these men would now be approaching his ninetieth birthday, and there are few comrades still alive to honour the memory of the hundreds of thousands who gave their lives so unquestioningly.

This is an appropriate time, therefore, to consider the extent to which the memorials of the First World War are being honoured and preserved, and the steps which may be necessary to ensure that the faith and patriotism of all those who fought in the war, survivors and fallen alike, are understood and commemorated beyond the lifetime of the last of their generation.

Unfortunately, many such memorials are in poor condition or have been destroyed completely. Shelters in Memorial Gardens have been demolished by vandals, crosses in remote villages have been pushed over, there are countless instances of memorials being defaced by graffiti, bronze name plaques have been stolen, carved inscriptions have almost disappeared over the years, churches have been deconsecrated and their memorials lost, and schools and factories have been demolished with similar results.

Prominent memorials have been used in recent years as a means to obtain publicity, or to make a political point. An I.R.A. bomb killed 11 people in Enniskillen on Remembrance Sunday, slogans such as "Fight war, not wars" were daubed on the Swansea monument and two women were arrested after writing, in red paint, the words "Dead men don't rape" across Bristol's memorial. For a while, until public reaction became universally hostile, so-called peace movements used white poppies as a means of putting across their political views.

The purpose of this book, with information about some three hundred First World War memorials in the U.K., is to draw attention to some which are in danger and also, by describing some of particular interest or merit, to try in some small measure to create interest in, and respect for, such memorials generally, with the possible result that they may eventually be more highly regarded, and therefore better protected and maintained.

Only memorials of the Great War have been considered and only those in Great Britain and Northern Ireland, rather than, for example, those in France or Belgium. In a very large number of cases the same memorial also commemorates the dead of the Second World War, but this is so common that it is not always specifically mentioned. The memorials described were in most instances visited during 1987.

Discussion about the form that war memorials should take began before the end of the war, and a major point of debate was the question of whether the most appropriate memorial was a monument of stone and bronze or something more utilitarian, such as a hospital, or memorial hall, or a scheme to provide funds for the families and children of the men who had died. It is easy to understand why so many felt that something of more apparent benefit to the community should be considered, but in fact, over the years, hospitals built in the early 1920's have frequently become outdated, and other such developments have also proved to have a comparatively limited life.

Of course, some towns and cities were able to afford both a permanent monument and also, for example, an assistance fund or a contribution to a local hospital. Other smaller communities, because of disagreement, built two memorials rather than compromise, the supporters of each scheme steadfastly ignoring the rival efforts.

1

In the autumn of 1919 the Royal Academy arranged a War Memorial Exhibition to assist promoters of such memorials and an advisory scheme was offered to all who wished to apply. All the works and designs exhibited had a direct reference to the war, and no utilitarian scheme was examined. There were models, photographs, designs and sketches, and actual statues, tablets, rolls of honour and stained glass. Works by Sir Edwin Lutyens and Sir Reginald Blomfield appeared several times in the catalogue, and, in the quadrangle, there was a model of the Great War Cross by Blomfield which was to be erected by the Imperial War Graves Commission in the war cemeteries abroad.

The type of memorial chosen was, of course, often determined by the amount of money raised. In most cases, the larger towns and cities had the more ambitious schemes for this reason, but there were many exceptions. For example, in Leeds, a city of almost half a million people, £6,000 was raised, while, in Loughborough, a population of just over 20,000 raised some £20,000.

Fund-raising efforts took many forms, and two interesting pieces of information about fund-raising for the Deptford war memorial appear in the records.

Examples exist of stamps which were apparently issued in support of the memorial. Slightly larger than normal postage stamps, they have the words

DEPTFORD WAR MEMORIAL 1914-1919

printed round the edges whilst in the centre are the coat of arms and battle scenes. Above the coat of arms are the words,

DULCE ET DECORUM EST PRO PATRIA MORI.

The second item appears in the Council Minutes, and shows that in June 1920 the Mayor was fined for running an illegal "Derby Draw" in aid of the memorial fund.

While the dates shown on memorials are most commonly 1914 and 1918, in a large number of cases 1914 and 1919 are chosen. Although fighting ceased in November 1918, the various peace treaties were not signed until much later, that with Germany being signed at Versailles on 28th June, 1919, five years to the day after the heir to the Austrian throne, Archduke Franz Ferdinand, was assassinated, and the drift to war began. "Peace Day" in Britain was officially 19th July, 1919 and on that day the Victory Parade took place.

The compiling of lists of names of the dead was a major task for war memorial committees, who often resorted to advertising for information in the local press. Often the criteria varied from city to city. Sometimes only those born in the city, or with their homes there, were considered, while on other occasions those, for example, whose parents lived there were included, and so on.

With such difficulties it is not surprising that some inaccuracies occurred. It was not impossible for a man's name to appear amongst the list of the fallen when he had, in fact, survived the war, and it was quite common for names to be omitted and added at a later, sometimes much later, date. For example, the name of Private William Bond was added to the memorial in Barrow, Cumbria, seventy years after his death at Ypres in 1917. An American relative compiling a family tree spotted that the name was missing and wrote to the local authority who, after investigation, rectified the mistake.

Names normally appear in alphabetical order but on occasions they are also divided into regiments or years or even sometimes, and this occurs most frequently in Scotland, in order of rank. It is usually very easy to see where names have originally been omitted because they then appear out of the normal order.

It was common for a man's name to appear on more than one type of memorial. He might be commemorated by an individual memorial and his name might then appear on the memorials of his school, university, church, club, place of work, regiment and community. The chapters of this book reflect these categories, and one example shown is that of Raymond Asquith, the son of the Prime Minister, whose name appears on the memorials at Winchester College, the Houses of Parliament and the village of Mells, where there is also an individual memorial to him.

Similarly, the name of the poet, Rupert Brooke, is on the memorials at Rugby School, at King's College, Cambridge, and in the churchyard of the village of Grantchester.

Memorials of the Great War take so many forms that it is perhaps not surprising that there are even memorials to animals. The Scottish National War Memorial in Edinburgh features tributes to animals, and in Lake on the Isle of Wight, a memorial was erected which incorporated a drinking trough

TO THE HORSES AND DOGS WHO ALSO BORE THE BURDEN AND HEAT

of the war.

An unusual memorial on the edge of the municipal golf course in Southampton has a stone inscribed,

WARRIOR. THIS WHITE GELDING, 16 HANDS, SERVED WITH THE OLD CONTEMPTIBLES IN FRANCE FROM 1914 TO THE END OF THE WAR. HE TOOK PART IN THE RETREAT FROM MONS AND WAS WOUNDED IN THE ADVANCE ON THE AISNE. AFTER THE SHRAPNEL HAD BEEN EXTRACTED HE RETURNED TO DUTY AND DID SERVICE IN SEVERAL FURTHER ACTIONS UNTIL THE ARMISTICE.

Chapter I

Memorials to Individuals

Most of the men who died in the First World War had no known graves, or were buried in war cemeteries near the battlefield. The Menin Gate at Ypres, designed by Sir Reginald Blomfield, records the names of some 50,000 missing dead of the battles in the area. The Somme Memorial at Thiepval, designed by Sir Edwin Lutyens, commemorates over 73,000 missing dead of the battle of the Somme. Amongst others is the Tyne Cot Memorial by Sir Herbert Baker, which records the names of 35,000 men who fell at Passchendaele and have no known graves. In addition, there are countless military cemeteries, large and small, where the dead are buried in individual graves marked by uniform headstones, on each of which are carved the man's regimental badge, symbol of religion, name, rank, date of death and age.

It is not surprising, therefore, that families or friends should, in many cases, have erected memorials to individuals in their home towns or villages. These memorials often took the form of a plaque or memorial window in a church although there are some examples of much more ambitious forms of commemoration.

As well as these expressions of family grief there were national memorials, either to dead heroes or heroines, or to individual war leaders who had contributed to the final victory.

The best-known individual memorial is that to the Unknown Warrior in Westminster Abbey. This combines the setting and treatment of a national memorial with the need which many families must have felt to have a focus for their grief. When the dead son or husband had no known grave, then the tomb in Westminster Abbey, with its truly "unknown" dead, went some way towards meeting that need.

The body of the Unknown Warrior had originally been selected in such a way that he could have been from any of the services and from any of the theatres of war. The body was then transported through France with the honours of a field marshal. Marshal Foch himself represented France at Boulogne where the coffin was put aboard the British destroyer *Verdun* which then crossed the channel with an escort of six further destroyers. The vessels reached Dover at 1 p.m. on 10th November, 1920, to a 10-gun salute from Dover Castle.

At Dover the coffin, covered by the Union Jack that had covered the coffin of Nurse Cavell, was transferred to a train which arrived at Victoria Station at nightfall, and there the body lay until the next morning.

1   *Funeral of the Unknown Warrior*

At 9.40 a.m. on the 11th November, 1920, the second anniversary of the Armistice, the coffin, on a gun carriage of the Royal Horse Artillery, and with a bearer party of Coldstream Guards, was taken by Hyde Park Corner and the Mall to Whitehall where the unveiling of the Cenotaph took place.

After that ceremony the funeral procession moved to Westminster Abbey, King George V walking immediately behind the coffin, followed by the Prince of Wales and other members of the Royal Family, and the Prime Minister.

2   *Funeral of the Unknown Warrior*

At the Abbey the twelve pall bearers included Lord Haig, Lord French and Lord Beatty, and 100 V.C.'s formed a guard of honour. On the coffin was a Union Jack, a side arm and a helmet, and the King's wreath of bay leaves and red roses with a card written by the King, "In proud memory of those who died unknown in the Great War. Unknown and yet well-known; as dying, and behold they live."

The King sprinkled French soil onto the coffin from a silver shell, and 100 sandbags of French soil were sent for the purpose of filling the grave.

The *Times* of 12th November wrote, "The Unknown Warrior whose body was to be buried may have been born to high position or to low; he may have been a sailor, a soldier or an airman; an Englishman, a Scotsman, a Welshman, an Irishman, a man of the Dominions, a Sikh, a Gurkha. No-one knows. But he was one who gave his life for the people of the British Empire."

One war leader who did not survive the conflict was Lord Kitchener. After campaigns in the Sudan, in Egypt and in South Africa he became Minister of War and led the successful campaign for voluntary recruiting at the start of the Great War ("Your Country Needs You"). He met his death when the cruiser *Hampshire* was sunk off Orkney in 1916, and he is commemorated in London both by a chapel and by a statue.

The chapel dedicated to Horatio Herbert, 1st Earl Kitchener of Khartoum and of Brooke in Kent is just inside one of the main entrances to St.

Paul's Cathedral. Unfortunately, for this reason, it has in the past been particularly vulnerable to vandalism and is now closed to the general public.

Inside the main doors to the chapel are iron gates through which the chapel could easily be viewed without further access, and it would seem possible to protect the chapel adequately without closing the outer doors and so preventing any view at all of the beautiful sculpture within. The fear expressed by the authorities that vagrants may use the space between the doors and the gates says little for the efficiency of the Cathedral's security arrangements and can hardly be taken seriously.

The chapel is notable for four fine pieces of sculpture by Reid Dick R.A. A recumbent marble figure of Kitchener himself dominates the centre of the chapel. Behind and above him are the figures of St. George, the Soldier of Christ, and St. Michael, the Standard Bearer, and on the opposite wall is a Pieta, all by the same artist.

Also within the chapel are housed, behind a wrought iron grille, the Rolls of Honour of the Royal Engineers, into which Kitchener himself had been commissioned in 1871.

The statue to Kitchener is a fine 1926 bronze by John Tweed and is sited against the Downing Street boundary of Horse Guards Parade. The pedestal is engraved
KITCHENER 1850–1916, ERECTED BY PARLIAMENT.

3   *Kitchener*

Not far from Kitchener's statue, on an island in the centre of the road opposite the Banqueting Hall in Whitehall, is a bronze equestrian statue of Douglas, Earl Haig, commander of the British army during most of the war years (see Plate C1, p.43).

4   *Haig:*
Edinburgh
Castle

On a stone pedestal, the statue by A. F. Hardiman was erected in 1937 and looks towards the Cenotaph further down Whitehall, and to the Houses of Parliament beyond.

In fact another statue of the Field Marshal, designed by George Wade, had been unveiled by the Lord Provost of Edinburgh fourteen years earlier, on 28th September, 1923. Also a bronze equestrian statue, on an irregular stone base on the Esplanade of Edinburgh Castle, it was, in fact, an individual commission. A plaque on the base gives the information that it was commissioned by Sir Dhumjibhoy Bomanzi of Bombay "in admiration of the services rendered to the British Empire by the Field Marshal."

Set into the ground between the fountains in Trafalgar Square, noticed by very few of the thousands who pass it daily, is an inscription stone which reads —

THESE FOUNTAINS AND THE BUSTS AGAINST THE NORTH WALL OF THE SQUARE WERE ERECTED BY PARLIAMENT TO THE MEMORY OF ADMIRALS OF THE FLEET EARL JELLICOE AND EARL BEATTY TO THE END THAT THEIR ILLUSTRIOUS SERVICES TO THE STATE MIGHT NEVER BE FORGOTTEN.

The busts are just below the level of the balustrade of the wall, and looking down Whitehall. That of Jellicoe, the Commander of the British Fleet during the First World War and at Jutland, is by William MacMillan who designed the Victory Medal, while that of Beatty, who accepted the surrender of the German Grand Fleet at Scapa Flow in 1918, is by Sir Charles Wheeler.

5   *Beatty*

5

6   *Edith Cavell, London*

7   *Edith Cavell, Norwich*

On a site close to the National Portrait Gallery and looking towards Trafalgar Square is a memorial to Nurse Edith Cavell.

At dawn on 12th October, 1915 she was executed by the Germans in Brussels for harbouring and assisting allied soldiers. At her court martial she admitted having helped 60 British and French soldiers and about 100 French and Belgian men of military age to escape to Holland. She had been matron of the Berkendael Medical Institute in Brussels, later a Red Cross Hospital.

The execution caused particular revulsion in Britain at the time and the memorial by Sir George Frampton was erected soon after the war's end, and unveiled by Queen Alexandra.

The monument incorporates a statue of the nurse and under it is carved

EDITH CAVELL. BRUSSELS. DAWN OCTOBER 12th 1915.

Also inscribed on the sides of the monument are the words —

HUMANITY, SACRIFICE, FORTITUDE and DEVOTION.

Edith Cavell's own words,

PATRIOTISM IS NOT ENOUGH. I MUST HAVE NO HATRED OR BITTERNESS FOR ANYONE.,

were added several years after the unveiling, and inscribed below the date of her execution.

Edith Cavell had been born on 4th December, 1865, at her father's vicarage at

8   *Edith Cavell's Grave*

Swardeston near Norwich, and in Norwich there are both a memorial to her and also her grave.

In October 1918, a month before the end of the war, Queen Alexandra unveiled a memorial on Tombland in Norwich. The memorial is a bronze bust of the nurse on a stone column, on the front of which a stone figure of a soldier holds up a laurel wreath in tribute. On the base of the memorial is inscribed
EDITH CAVELL, NURSE, PATRIOT AND MARTYR.
The memorial was the work of Henry Pegram.

The large Georgian building behind the memorial, now part of a hotel, became, after the war, the Cavell Home of the Norwich District Nursing Association.

The body of Edith Cavell was re-interred on Life's Green beside Norwich Cathedral, on May 15th, 1919, after a memorial service in Westminster Abbey.

Her remains had left Brussels on the 13th, and a gun carriage had borne her coffin through the streets of the Belgian capital. A religious ceremony had been held at the Gare du Nord before the coffin had been placed in the train for Ostend en route for Dover, London and Norwich, and a final service in the Cathedral there.

Private memorials erected by individuals' families were most commonly placed in the local church or churchyard.

In St. Mary's Church at Wargrave, in Berkshire, there are several wall-plaque memorials to individuals killed in the war. One is to Lt. Colonel Spencer-Watson, V.C., D.S.O. who fell at Rosignol (sic) Wood on 28th March 1918, commanding the 5th Battalion King's Own Yorkshire Light Infantry. For his heroism that day he was awarded the posthumous Victoria Cross. Another is to Captain Beresford-Chancellor, of the 7th Royal Berkshires, who died from wounds in Salonica on Christmas Eve 1916, aged 21.

10   *Clipston, Northamptonshire*

A third is to the memory of Captain Lionel Sydney Platt of the 17th Lancers, attached to the Royal Flying Corps, who died in aerial combat north-east of Vitry-en-Artois, in France, on 13th April, 1917.

Finally there is one to Arthur Alexander Austen-Leigh, a captain in the 4th Royal Berkshire Regiment, killed near Albert in France in 1918. He was the youngest son of the Reverend A. H. Austen-Leigh, a great-nephew of Jane Austen and vicar of Wargrave for many years.

Also in the church is a plaque to all the men of the Parish who served in the war, a window and chancel screen in memory of the fallen, and a window as thanksgiving for the restoration of peace in 1918. Finally, on the beautiful green across which the church is approached is a stone memorial designed by Sir Edwin Lutyens.

In the parish church of Clipston, in Northamptonshire, there is a memorial tablet to thirteen men of the village who died in the 1914–18 war. One of these, Lieut. C. R. A. Wartnaby of the Northamptonshire Yeomanry, who was killed in action at Neuve Chapelle on 11th March, 1915, also has within the church an individual memorial with an unusual feature. This is a crucifix which was found on the battlefield of Neuve Chapelle and sent to Clipston Church, as a memorial, by one of the friends of the dead man.

Holy Trinity Church, Guildford, contains the regimental chapel and the war memorial of the Queen's Regiment, and amongst the individual memorials there is a brass plaque to

9   *Wargrave, Berkshire*

![Memorial plaque at Guildford, Holy Trinity Church]

11   *Guildford, Holy Trinity Church*

12   *Horner Memorial*

the memory of Dawson Warren, Lieutenant Colonel of the 1st Battalion the Queen's Regiment, and son of Major General D. S. Warren. He was killed at Paissy on the Aisne, on 17th September, 1914, while in command of his battalion.

The Church of St. Andrew in the village of Mells in Somerset has, to the left of the chancel, what used to be the Lady Chapel, but later became the Horner Chapel, containing the Horner family vault, and marble plaques to some of those buried below.

In the centre of the chapel, and dominating it, is a bronze equestrian statue of Edward Horner, the last direct male heir to the Horner Estate. A Lieutenant in the 18th Hussars, he died of wounds at Noyelles on 21st November, 1917, in the Battle of Cambrai.

His only brother had died before the war, and in September 1916 his sister, who eventually inherited the family estate, was widowed when her husband, Raymond Asquith, son of the Prime Minister, was killed whilst serving as a lieutenant in the Grenadier Guards.

The statue of Edward Horner is the work of Sir Alfred Munnings and is said to be the first horse sculpture by this famous painter of horses. As a result of this work he was asked by the Jockey Club Members to make a statue of Brown Jack for the Epsom course.

The base of the memorial at Mells was designed by Sir Edwin Lutyens and set into it is the cross which marked Horner's grave in France.

Also in the chapel is the cross which marked the grave in France of Raymond Asquith. Elsewhere, on the south wall of the church, is a memorial to him, with lettering by Eric Gill and a bronze wreath above by Lutyens.

A further connection of the church with the First World War is the grave in the churchyard of the famous war poet Siegfried Sassoon. His last wish was to be buried near Ronald Knox, the priest and scholar who for some years lived at the Manor nearby.

In St. Mary's Church in Kettlewell, in Wharfedale, is a memorial window commemorating one of the dead of the First World War. A nearby tablet is inscribed,

THE EAST WINDOW WAS ERECTED IN MEMORY OF CHARLES GODFREY HAGGAS CUTCLIFFE HYNE, A LIEUTENANT IN THE IRISH GUARDS WHO, AT THE AGE OF 18, ON NOVEMBER 21st 1916 GAVE HIS LIFE FOR THIS ENGLAND.

He had gone straight from Rugby School to a commission in the Irish Guards arranged for him by his godmother, Lady Harmsworth, and had been badly wounded on the 15th September, 1916, during the Battle of the Somme, in an action in which his unit sustained 17 casualties out of 25 men. He died two months later in a London hospital and was taken home to Kettlewell and buried with full military honours. Present were three fellow officers, two drummers and eight N.C.O.'s, as pall bearers.

In the parish church of All Saints in the village of Mattersey, in Nottinghamshire, is a memorial window to three sons of the Huntriss family who lived at Mattersey Hall at the time of the First World War. The window is divided into three, each part showing the figure of a medieval youth in armour either kneeling or looking upwards towards an image of Christ holding a crown in front of him (see Plate C2, p.43).

At the top of the window are the words —
BE THOU FAITHFUL UNTO DEATH AND I WILL GIVE THEE A CROWN OF LIFE,
while the inscription at the foot of the window reads
IN EVER LOVING MEMORY OF LIEUT. WILLIAM HUNTRISS, 3RD DUKE OF WELLINGTON'S WEST RIDING REGIMENT (ATTACHED TO GOLD COAST REGT.) BORN DECEMBER 16th 1886. DIED OCTOBER 23rd 1918 AT COOMASSIE, AFRICA.
CAPT. HAROLD EDWARDS HUNTRISS. 1st BATTALION BEDFORDSHIRE REGIMENT. BORN MAY 23rd 1890. DIED OF WOUNDS AT FESTHUBERT, FRANCE. MAY 17th 1915.
CAPT. CYRIL JOHN HUNTRISS 1st BATTALION EAST YORKSHIRE REGIMENT. BORN JANUARY 29th 1893. KILLED AT FRICOURT, FRANCE. JULY 1st 1916. THE THREE SONS OF WILLIAM HUNTRISS, LATE OF MATTERSEY HALL, AND CHARLOTTE ELIZABETH HIS WIFE.
THE LORD GAVE AND THE LORD HATH TAKEN AWAY. BLESSED BE THE NAME OF THE LORD.

Mattersey Hall is now a Bible College but from 1947 until 1972 was a boys' preparatory school, and one old boy, Mike Garrs, remembers that the custom on Remembrance Day was for each boy to place his poppy on the ledge under the Huntriss window at the end of the service in church.

He was fascinated by the memorial even as an eight-year old and on leaving the school for Uppingham School was surprised to find the names of the Huntriss brothers, along with those of some four hundred others, commemorated on the walls of the Uppingham Great War Memorial Chapel. William Huntriss Junior had been in the shooting team at Uppingham and gone on to become a solicitor; Harold Edwards Huntriss went on to the Royal Military College at Sandhurst and was a regular soldier at the outbreak of war; and Cyril John Huntriss had a distinguished school career, being a school praeposter, and in the school rugby, hockey and

running teams. In the war he won the Military Cross and was mentioned in dispatches.

The Huntriss window in All Saints Church is still a beautiful and moving memorial, but unfortunately time has not been kind to that part of the church and the stonework in many places, including that around the window, is badly weathered, almost to the point where the window may be endangered.

A family grave in Springbank Cemetery, Aberdeen, has a gravestone which gives the sad history of one family's losses in the Great War.

Captain Harry Brooke and his wife, of Fairly, an estate near Kingswells a few miles west of Aberdeen, had five sons and two daughters. One of the sons died in infancy and the eldest surviving son joined the Gordon Highlanders, his father's old regiment, after gaining the Sword of Honour whilst at Sandhurst.

This son, Captain James Anson Otho Brooke, was serving with the 2nd Battalion Gordon Highlanders at Gheluvelt in Belgium early in the war, on 29th October, 1914, when he led a counter-attack, in desperate circumstances, of about 100 men hastily gathered together, including cooks and signallers. Brooke was killed, but for his bravery and leadership was posthumously awarded the V.C.

The third son, Captain Henry B. Brooke was wounded leading his men in the great charge of the Gordons at Mametz on July 1st, 1916, and he died shortly afterwards on July 24th.

On May 25th, 1917, the Brookes' youngest son, Sub-Lieut. Patrick H. Brooke, died from enteric fever while on active service with the Royal Navy.

One final blow to the family was the death of their son-in-law, Captain Napier Cameron of the Cameron Highlanders. The husband of their daughter Constance, he was killed in the battle of the Aisne, leaving her with a baby daughter.

The only son to survive the war, Captain Arthur Brooke of the 18th Lancers, was wounded at Mons but recovered, and later resumed his career with the Indian Army. He died in 1951. The father, Captain Harry Brooke, was ultimately knighted for services to his regiment, and died in 1921.

At the foot of the headstone in Springbank Cemetery is a rough wooden cross which originally marked the spot in Belgium where Otho, the son who gained the V.C., fell and was initially buried.

In addition to the family grave, the war memorial in front of the Parish Church at Kingswells also commemorates the names of the Brookes' dead, inscribed along with the names of the others of the village who gave their lives.

The memorial cross in the churchyard of St. Martin's Church in Ashton-on-Mersey was unveiled by Henry Adams Gray who had lost three sons in the war.

A family grave shows that his wife died in 1914, his son Percy, of the Royal Fusiliers, died aged 23 on 25th August, 1916, and his sons William, aged 40 and Leonard, aged 30, of the Royal Welsh Fusiliers died within 3 weeks of each

13   *Brooke Memorial, Aberdeen*

14 *Cartland Memorial, Tewkesbury Abbey*

HIS BROTHERS NORMAN CAIRNS ROBERTSON, CAPT. 2nd BATT. HAMPSHIRE REGT. WHO DIED 20th JUNE 1917 AT HANOVER, GERMANY, AND OF LAURANCE GRANT ROBERTSON 2nd LIEUT. 2nd BATTALION KINGS OWN SCOTTISH BORDERERS WHO WAS KILLED IN ACTION IN FRANCE DURING THE BATTLE OF THE SOMME IN OR NEAR DELVILLE WOOD 30th JULY 1916.

In Clovelly in Devon, on a beautiful site high above the sea, close to the point where the narrow lane starts to wind down to the village, is a stone cross on a cobble base. Erected by Christine Hamblyn, it is to the memory of her brother John Manners, a Lieutenant in the Grenadier Guards, who was killed at Villers Cotterets on 1st September, 1914.

Memorials to individuals are sometimes to be found in their former schools or universities. Memorials at Harrow, Beverley and Clare College are described in a later chapter.

Amongst many individual memorial plaques at Eton College, most of them in the cloisters, is one to the three grandsons of the Rev. Charles Old Goodford, a former Provost of Eton College. Frank Middleton, a captain in the Dorset Regiment, died at Sahil in the Persian Gulf on 17th November, 1914, aged 37 years; Ernest Middleton, a 2nd Lieutenant in the Dorset Yeomanry, died in Egypt on 26th February, 1916, aged 28; and Charles J. H. Goodford M.C., a Lieutenant in the Hampshire Regiment, died on the Somme on 1st July, 1916, aged 20.

other in February and March 1919, presumably from wounds.

Just inside the entrance gates to the grounds of Tewkesbury Abbey is a family memorial. A crucifix on a stone base, it records the death of James Bertram Falkner Cartland in the First World War, and of his two sons on successive days in the Second.

James Cartland, a Major in the Worcestershire Regiment was killed in action on 27th May, 1918 at Berry-au-Bac, aged 42.

His son, James, a Captain in the Lincolnshire Regiment, was killed aged 27 on 29th May, 1940, two days after the anniversary of the earlier death, and on the following day, 30th May, 1940, Ronald, a Major in the Worcestershire Yeomanry, was killed aged 33.

Finally the memorial records the death of Mary Hamilton Cartland 1877-1976, "With courage never to submit or yield."

There are, of course, many memorials unconnected with the individual's former church.

On the Downs near Dunstable is a beauty spot named Robertson Corner which is, in fact, a war memorial to two individuals, brothers who died in the war within a year of each other. The commemorative stone and plaque are quite insignificant, despite their position in a fork in the road, and can easily be passed un-noticed.

The plaque reads,

ROBERTSON CORNER WAS BEQUEATHED TO THE NATIONAL TRUST BY W. A. ROBERTSON IN MEMORY OF

15 *Manners Memorial, Clovelly*

16   *Mobbs Memorial, Northampton*

Another is to Montague Aubrey Cholmeley, Baronet, a Captain in the Grenadier Guards, killed at Festubert on 24th December, 1914, aged 38; Hugh Valentine Cholmeley, a 2nd Lieutenant in the Grenadier Guards, killed at Ypres on 7th April, 1916, aged 28; and Harry Lewin Cholmeley, a Lieutenant in the Border Regiment, killed at Beaumont-Hamel on 1st July, 1916, aged 23.

The names of the two Guards Officers appear also on a further memorial inscribed,

TO THE GLORY OF GOD AND IN PROUD REMEMBRANCE OF 96 OLD ETONIANS OF THE GRENADIER GUARDS WHO LAID DOWN THEIR LIVES FOR KING AND COUNTRY IN THE WAR OF 1914-1918. THIS TABLET IS ERECTED BY THEIR ETONIAN BROTHER OFFICERS.

The names are listed below the inscription.

An interesting memorial from a war almost 70 years later is that to Colonel "H" Jones V.C. who died in the Falklands.

The memorial in Northampton to Lieut. Colonel Edgar Mobbs, was originally unveiled by Lord Lilford in July 1921 in the Market Place, and later moved in 1937 to the Garden of Remembrance in Abington Square (see Plate C3, p.43).

The monument, with its bronze bust of Mobbs and panels of scenes from the battlefield and the rugby pitch, surmounted by a bronze figure of the Goddess of Fame, is however, only part of the way in which Edgar Mobbs is commemorated.

In 1921 the first Mobbs Memorial match between the East Midlands and the Barbarians rugby teams was held and, almost seventy years later, the match is still an annual event.

Edgar Mobbs, in the years before the war, had captained the Saints, Northampton's rugby team, had played for the Barbarians, and had been capped for England on seven occasions.

At the outbreak of war he raised a "Sportsman's Battalion", officially the 7th Battalion Northamptonshire Regiment, and as a Lieutenant Colonel eventually died in an attack at Passchendaele.

Each year before the match there is a short ceremony, and a wreath in Saints or Barbarians colours is laid at the Mobbs Memorial.

In 1915 the artist Stanley Spencer joined the R.A.M.C. as an orderly, and shortly afterwards was posted to Macedonia where he ultimately served with the Berkshire Regiment.

In 1922 he started work on designs for a series of mural paintings depicting scenes from his war experiences, and these were seen by Mr. and Mrs. Behrend who undertook to build a chapel to house the finished work.

The chapel was built at Burghclere, near Newbury, between 1923 and 1927, to the designs of Lionel Pearson, instructed by Spencer. It was dedicated on 25th March, 1927, as the Oratory of All Souls, subsequently becoming known as the Sandham Memorial Chapel in memory of Mrs. Behrend's brother H. W. Sandham, who had died in 1919 from illness whilst serving in Macedonia. The chapel was given to the National Trust by the Behrends in 1947 and remains in its ownership today.

The 19 paintings in the chapel were executed by Spencer between 1927 and 1932. The best known, perhaps, *The Resurrection of the Soldiers,* dominates the chapel, taking up the whole of the east wall opposite the entrance door and behind the altar. This painting alone took the artist nearly a year to complete. As a whole, the cycle emphasizes the everyday incidents of army life rather than the horrors of the trenches, and the other 18 paintings include such scenes as *Convoy arriving with Wounded, Kit*

11

17   *Sandham Memorial, Burghclere*

18
*Spencer's
'Resurrection',
Burghclere*

Inspection, Reveille and *Map-Reading.*

Of course, individual memorials of the scale of that at Burghclere are not commonplace. Fortunately, the modesty of a particular memorial does not make it less valid.

The father of Mr. E. W. Himsworth of Scarborough was killed in the last months of the war when his son was only 6 years old. Mr. Himsworth's only recollection of his father was when he was home on leave, at the time that he himself was only about four.

Some years ago the Church of the Transfiguration in Albert Avenue, Hull, Mr. Himsworth's former home town, was scheduled for demolition and by chance he was informed that several brass memorial plaques to individual soldiers had been removed, and that near relatives, on proof of identity, could claim them. Any unclaimed plaques would be buried in consecrated ground. One apparently commemorated Mr. Himsworth's father, although he had not been aware of its existence, and so he duly claimed it.

The plaque is about 8ins. by 2ins. and inscribed,

PTE T. HIMSWORTH, SHROPS. L.I. WHO FELL IN FRANCE. AUG. 22. 1918.

It is now mounted on a triangular block of attractively grained wood and proudly displayed along with a small framed photograph of the soldier, and a poppy which is replaced each year.

19   *Himsworth Plaque*

Chapter II

Schools and Universities

Of all the many school memorials to the dead of the First World War, that at Winchester College, in the form of a beautiful cloister designed by Sir Herbert Baker, the architect of the Bank of England, was immediately recognised in 1924 as one of the finest war memorials in the country.

The arches round the central Garth are rounded and resting on pairs of simple pillars. The inner walls are faced with local flint and although Portland stone is used for most of the stonework the name tablets on the inner walls are made of Derbyshire Hopton-Wood stone, the tiles of the roof are of Purbeck stone and the paths which intersect the Garth are set with old London paving-stone. Where the paths meet in the centre is a cross protected by two crusader figures, this monument being the work of Alfred Turner.

On the tablets are inscribed the names of five hundred Wykehamists who fell in the war. There are sixteen tablets grouped in pairs, each pair being linked by a stone recording the great battles of the war. The names of those commemorated are listed by the year in which they came to Winchester and their rank, regiment and place of death are also recorded.

For example, the name of the Prime Minister's son, Raymond Asquith, is listed under 1892, when he came to the college, and he was killed at Trones Wood when a Lieutenant in the Grenadier Guards.

In addition to the name tablets, the Cloister is decorated by the arms and badges of many regiments and allied countries, amongst other carvings, and at each of the four corners is a dome dedicated to the three great Dominions and to India. A long inscription of stone letters runs right round the Cloister in a continuous band 9ft. from the ground and reads,

THANKS BE TO GOD FOR THE SERVICE OF THE FIVE HUNDRED WYKEHAMISTS WHO WERE FOUND FAITHFUL UNTO DEATH AMID THE MANIFOLD CHANCES OF THE GREAT WAR. IN THE DAY OF BATTLE THEY FORGAT NOT GOD, WHO CREATED THEM TO DO HIS WILL, NOR THEIR COUNTRY, THE STRONGHOLD OF FREEDOM, NOR THEIR SCHOOL, THE MOTHER OF GODLINESS AND DISCIPLINE. STRONG IN THIS THREEFOLD FAITH THEY WENT FORTH FROM HOME AND KINDRED TO THE BATTLEFIELDS OF THE WORLD, AND TREADING THE PATH OF DUTY AND SACRIFICE LAID DOWN THEIR LIVES FOR MANKIND.
THOU THEREFORE, FOR WHOM THEY DIED, SEEK NOT THINE OWN, BUT SERVE AS THEY SERVED, AND IN PEACE OR IN WAR BEAR THYSELF EVER AS CHRIST'S SOLDIER, GENTLE IN ALL THINGS, VALIANT IN ACTION, STEADFAST IN ADVERSITY.

As well as the building of the War Cloister, the memorial fund of the college provided for a new stone altar in the chapel, the reconstruction of the reredos, four memorial volumes, and the full provision of any assistance needed during the whole of their school life for sons of Wykehamists who lost their lives in the war.

At Rugby School, the stone of the attractive War Memorial Chapel, which looks across the famous Close, is in contrast to the brick of the earlier school buildings.

Inside the chapel is a beautiful cabinet decorated with carving and marquetry and

20   *A Corner of Winchester Cloisters*

21 *Rugby School Chapel*

supported by carved columns. It is octagonal in shape and eight shallow, glass-fronted drawers contain the volumes of the War Register.

Surmounting this impressive piece is the fine bronze of a young officer with hands clasped before him and head bowed, and on the walls beside the cabinet are carved the names of those commemorated.

The Great War Memorial Chapel at Uppingham School, off the main chapel building, was designed by Ernest Newton R.A., one of his last works before his death in 1922. This beautiful octagonal shrine has approximately four hundred names inscribed on the stone panels of its walls in gold lettering,

amongst them the names of the three Huntriss brothers whose memorial window is in All Saints Church in Mattersey (see Plate C4, p.43).

A bronze plaque at one end of the Arcade at Eton College is inscribed,

1914–1919. THE NAMES RECORDED HERE ARE THOSE OF THE 1157 ETONIANS WHO DIED IN THE WAR IN WHICH 5660 SERVED. LET US ALWAYS REMEMBER THEIR VALOUR AND THEIR SACRIFICE WITH LOVE AND THANKFULNESS AND PRAY GOD TO MAKE US WORTHY OF THEM IN TIME TO COME.

The names are then inscribed on panels along the Arcade and to them have subsequently been added those from the Second World War.

The memorial at Harrow School is the War Memorial Building designed by Sir Herbert

22 *Rugby School Memorial*

15

23
*Eton College
Memorial*

Baker, the architect of Winchester's Cloister. The memorial's external architecture closely reflects that of the surrounding buildings of the school.

The main feature of the memorial is the Shrine on the ground floor where the names of over 600 Old Boys and Masters who fell in the war are carved into the walls, and roof bosses bear the arms of England, Harrow School and France, to represent the places of birth, education and death of the fallen.

A stone altar at one end has carved above it, in the curved wall of a niche, the inscription

O VALIANT HEARTS WHO TO YOUR GLORY CAME, THROUGH DUST OF CONFLICT AND THROUGH BATTLE FLAME, TRANQUIL YOU LIE YOUR KNIGHTLY VIRTUE PROVED, YOUR MEMORY HALLOWED IN THE LAND YOU LOVED.

On the first floor of the building, one of the rooms is dedicated to the memory of 2nd Lieutenant Alex Fitch of the Royal Garrison Artillery, who died on 18th September, 1918, at the age of 19. His parents, Sir Cecil and Lady Fitch, gave the room, with its furniture and fittings, and a portrait of their son hangs above the Tudor fireplace. Although the room dates only from 1926, the furniture and fittings are antique, the panelling being Tudor and the floor timbers made from the *St. Vincent,* a Georgian Warship. The table in the centre of the room is Cromwellian. To quote from the schools' own description,

THE ROOM IS HISTORY, ITS INSPIRATION WAS MEMORY, BUT ITS PURPOSE IS FOR TODAY AND TOMORROW.

In the room are kept copies of the six

24   *Harrow
School
Memorial*

volumes of the Book of Remembrance of the school. The entries are in order of date of death, and there is a short biography and photograph of each of the fallen.

The Shrine was dedicated by Randall Davidson, the Archbishop of Canterbury, and the War Memorial was opened in 1926 by Mr. Stanley Baldwin, the Prime Minister. Both men were themselves Old Harrovians.

The dedication of a Cross in memory of the old boys and masters of the Dragon School, Oxford, who gave their lives during the Great War, was performed by the Bishop of Oxford on 8th November 1920.

The names of the 83 who died were read out at the service, and their names are inscribed on a Celtic cross erected on a high bank by the Cherwell, and on the edge of the playing fields.

The War Memorial Committee met as early as March 7th, 1918, and a letter was sent out in October of that year appealing for subscriptions, and enclosing suggested designs for a granite cross, these designs having been prepared by

C. Lynam, the father of the then headmaster and "author of many works on archaeology, and an expert student of old crosses."

On the Green above Llandaff Cathedral, Cardiff, is the war memorial to the First World War dead of the Parish and of the Cathedral School.

The memorial has three impressive bronze figures by the Llandaff sculptor Goscombe John, who was also responsible for a number of works within the cathedral, and the nearby figure of Archdeacon Buckley. The centre of the memorial's three figures has one arm raised in blessing whilst holding a shield in the other. It is flanked by the figure of a schoolboy in shorts and rugby boots and with a rifle slung over his shoulder, and by that of a workman, perhaps a miner, with sleeves rolled up and with a rifle by his side.

On the plinth beneath the central figure is the inscription

LLANDAFF REMEMBERS HER OWN SONS AND THOSE OF THE CATHEDRAL SCHOOL WHO GAVE THEIR LIVES IN THE GREAT WAR.

27 *The Llandaff Memorial*

This statue stands in a niche in the wall and to one side of it is a plaque

IN COMMEMORATION OF OUR BROTHER
LAURENTIANS WHO FELL IN THE GREAT WAR.

Sixty-nine names follow. A matching plaque for the dead of the Second War is on the other side of the statue.

A bronze memorial tablet listing the pupils of Wintringham Grammar School who had died during the First World War, was placed after the war in a glass-fronted case on the wall of the old school premises in Eleanor Street, Grimsby.

A similar tablet was provided after the Second World War, but in the early fifties the school buildings were closed and the tablets were moved to St. Luke's Church where a service for the Hallowing of the memorials in their new resting place was held on 5th May, 1954.

The church building in turn, however, was closed, and eventually demolished. Once more it was necessary to move the tablets, this time to the new school buildings on the outskirts of Grimsby where they have been fixed to the wall near the main entrance door to the school.

Credit is due to the ex-servicemen who, by their perseverance, have made sure that the memorials have survived and, indeed, they have even arranged for plaques on the original school site in Eleanor Street to record the progressive re-sitings of the memorials.

Beneath the workman are inscribed the names of 57 Parishioners, 56 men and 1 woman, Edith Mary Tonkin V.A.D., while under the schoolboy are listed a similar number of names from the Cathedral School.

One old boy of the school, Leonard Lean, remembers when it was necessary to walk slowly and with cap off if passing in front of the memorial, while it was permissible to run or wear a cap if using the road behind it.

The memorial is a particularly beautiful one, with its fine sculpture and its situation between the school and cathedral, looking out across flower beds and the well-tended Green.

In Beverley Minster is a war memorial plaque with a coat of arms and the inscription

TO THE GLORY OF GOD AND IN MEMORY OF THE
FOLLOWING OLD BOYS OF BEVERLEY GRAMMAR
SCHOOL WHO MADE THE SUPREME SACRIFICE IN THE
GREAT WAR 1914-1918.

The names of 29 men follow, including two brothers whose personal memorial tablet is also in the Minster. It is to the memory of 2nd Lieutenant Philip Green of the East Yorkshire Regiment who died on 28th March, 1918, and his brother Frank, a Lieutenant in the Yorkshire Regiment, who died exactly three months earlier, at Passchendaele, on 28th December, 1917.

In the main hall of Lawrence Sheriff School, Rugby, is a memorial to the old boys who were killed in the First World War. It is a statue of St. George slaying the dragon, under which is the inscription

THERE ARE DRAGONS STILL. 1914-1918.

28 *Beverley Minster Memorial*

THERE ARE DRAGONS STILL
1914 – 1918

29   *Lawrence Sheriff School Memorial*

Another bronze tablet commemorating the dead of the Great War is to be found inside the entrance of Fishergate County Primary School in York.

At the time of the war it was known as Fishergate Council School, and the then headmaster, Mr. G. T. Barker, kept a most detailed and comprehensive school log. This covered not only all the activities of the school, but also included press cuttings and pieces of information about old boys and masters of the school.

Naturally, once the war started, its influence on the entries in the log was considerable. The entry of 17th August, 1914, notes that the school had been requisitioned by the War Office and this remained so until 31st October, during which time the school shared premises with another.

On 4th September the entry read, "Mr. G. L. Rea has volunteered and been accepted for active service in response to Lord Kitchener's appeal." He was replaced by another teacher who in turn volunteered.

On 21st September the school field was commandeered for military purposes.

On 13th October, 1914, the first note of the death of an old boy is found, Sergeant Alexander Hutchison of the Cameron Highlanders being killed on 25th September on the Aisne. Similar reports then followed in quick succession on 23rd October, 28th October, 9th November, 24th

November and 29th November, making six in six weeks.

Not only deaths were reported, but any information from the newspapers about old boys in the war, or photographs sent by the men themselves (and in one case a poem), were all put into the log.

On 1st June, 1915, it was recorded that Reginald Sadler had been commissioned in the 17th Northumberland Fusiliers. "This makes the 5th old boy who has been made an officer in the army."

In amongst all the entries about the war and the deaths of old boys, more normal information is given about medical examinations and school register inspections.

On 10th July, 1916, there is a reference to the school making sandbags for the war effort, and there are many entries concerning fund-raising activities.

On 12th July, 1917, the summer holidays had an extra day added to celebrate the victory at Messines on 7th June when old boy Leslie Gardner won the Military Medal.

The final entry about a fatality was some weeks after the armistice. On 28th December, 1918, it was noted that news had been received that Wallace Eland M.M., a prisoner of war, had died in captivity.

In May 1919 there was a "Welcome Home" party for old boys, and the names of the 76 who fell were read out. It was estimated that 470 old boys had fought, and of them 20 had been commissioned and, amongst other decorations, 9 Military Medals, 6 D.C.M.'s, 1 D.F.C., 2 Medailles Militaires and 1 Croix de Guerre had been received.

Perhaps the most impressive university memorial, certainly in scale, is the Memorial Court of Clare College, Cambridge. The entrance arch to the courtyard contains plaques with the names of the dead of both the First and the Second World Wars, and the First World War list is headed

TO THE IMMORTAL MEMORY OF THOSE MEN OF CLARE COLLEGE WHO AT THE CALL OF KING AND COUNTRY LEFT ALL THAT WAS DEAR TO THEM, ENDURED HARDNESS, FACED DANGER AND FINALLY PASSED OUT OF THE SIGHT OF MEN BY THE PATH OF DUTY AND SELF SACRIFICE GIVING UP THEIR OWN LIVES THAT OTHERS MIGHT LIVE IN FREEDOM, LET THOSE WHO COME AFTER SEE TO IT THAT THEIR NAMES BE NOT FORGOTTEN.

Above one of the entrances at Clare College Memorial Court is an individual memorial to Wilfred Saxby Barham, a Captain in the Buffs, who died of wounds on 10th October, 1915, aged 20. The memorial is inscribed "Love by Life, Love by Death, is tried. Live ye for England. He for England died."

The memorial in the Chapel at Magdalene College, Cambridge, consists of a metal tablet under the south-eastern window and a silver-gilt altar cross.

The tablet was dedicated by the Bishop of Ely on Armistice Day 1923 and was designed by Mr. Alexander Fisher. Adorned with an armorial shield and the dates 1914 and 1918 in enamel, it carries the names and regiments of 65 members

30   *Clare College Memorial Court*

of the college, 11 of whom have "M.C." after their name (see Plate C5, p.44).

The altar cross designed by Mr. Omar Ramsden is inscribed PORTUM NACTIS 'To those who have gained the haven'.

The war memorial of King's College, Cambridge is also in the Chapel, to one side of the high altar. Previously the chantry chapel of John Argentain, Provost in the early 16th century, it was converted in 1920-21 into a 1914-18 war memorial to members of the college and named All Saints Memorial Chapel.

On one side of the chapel are engraved the names, in categories, of the Fellows, Scholars, Choral Scholars, Pensioners, Choristers, Boys of the Choir School and College Servants who fell in the war.

Amongst the list of Fellows is the name of Rupert Brooke, whose name also appears on the churchyard memorial at nearby Grantchester.

Magdalen College, Oxford, had, after the First World War, two memorials. One was a tall cross inscribed only "1914" in front and "1918" on the back, and erected by the west door of the

31   *King's College Memorial*

Chapel. It was felt sad by some that the beautiful grass of the quadrangle had been sacrificed to stone paving around the memorial, and when the memorial was moved in the Second World War it was never restored, and eventually given on "permanent loan" to the village of Wheatley.

The second memorial, existing still, is in a passageway at the entrance to the cloister. The names of all who served, 206 names arranged alphabetically with regiments, and battle honours, are on tablets on the walls. Unfortunately the darkness of the passage makes it difficult for the memorial to be very effective though nearby, and in a better light, is another plaque inscribed

HAVE IN HONOUR YOU WHO ENTER HERE ALL THOSE SONS OF THIS HOUSE WHO WENT FORTH TO SERVE IN THE YEARS 1914-1918.

At Keble College, Oxford, there is a most attractive memorial shrine to the side of the entrance to the Chapel. The names of 175 men are set in oak panelling and a cornice is inscribed with Bunyan's words,

SO THEY PASSED OVER AND ALL THE TRUMPETS SOUNDED FOR THEM ON THE OTHER SIDE.

The shrine is enclosed by a grille and opposite the door is a panel incorporating the two soldier saints, St. George and St. Martin. Under this panel is a glass case containing a Book of Remembrance.

The Edinburgh University war memorial was unveiled on 19th February 1923 by the Chancellor and on the 5th November 1953 the then Chancellor, the Duke of Edinburgh, unveiled the Second World War addition.

The memorial, with its large bronze name tablets, is at the western end of the Old Quad facing the entrance to the Quad. Despite what should be a prominent position the memorial is difficult to see except at very close range because it is hidden by pillars and also in poor light as a result.

The main inscription reads —

TO THE GLORIOUS MEMORY OF THE ALUMNI OF THIS UNIVERSITY WHO FELL IN THE GREAT WAR.

Almost 1000 names of the fallen are recorded on the memorial.

32 *Keble College Memorial*

Chapter III

Churches, Clubs and Places of Work

In almost every case the name of a man who fell in the war was recorded as part of the memorial of his village or town, and inscribed either on a monument or on a Roll of Honour.

Memorials at his place of worship, relaxation or employment, therefore, tended to be a form of duplication, as indeed were those of regiment or school.

Nevertheless, they were an important source of consolation to the families and friends of the dead, and the only opportunity, in some cases, to pay a more personal tribute to the sacrifices made. The name of the man, along with a score of others, on a plaque in his parish church, might well seem to have more relevance than on a Roll of Honour, containing several thousand names, in a city centre.

In smaller communities the church was often the site of the general war memorial, either inside the building or in the form of a churchyard cross, and in the case of many villages no other memorial would exist.

In other instances, however, normally in larger towns and cities, a memorial in a church would be purely to commemorate its former members.

The church of St. Nathanial's, Edge Hill, Liverpool, was officially closed in June 1981. At least this church, one of many inner city churches which have been de-consecrated in recent years, has avoided demolition and today houses a shed-building business.

Inside the building various memorial tablets still remain, including one inscribed,

TO THE GLORY OF GOD AND IN AFFECTIONATE REMEMBRANCE OF THE MEN FROM ST. NATHANIAL'S CHURCH AND PARISH WHO MADE THE SUPREME SACRIFICE IN THE GREAT WAR 1914-1919.

The war memorial is surrounded by timber, stacked on the floor and against walls, but the owner of the business is sympathetic and his employees are helpful, and reasonable access is possible. Of the 104 men named on the memorial one is a V.C., D. Jones, and another is J. H. Theobald whose son has been campaigning, so far without success, for the removal of the plaque to a more appropriate location.

With the passage of time and with movements of population, it is easy to see why churches sometimes become redundant, but surely the church authorities, who receive the proceeds from the disposal of the buildings, could give some thought to the re-siting of war memorials which are affected. Individual memorials are perhaps a different matter, but parish war memorials should surely be protected.

The memorial in the churchyard of Holy Trinity Church, Cambridge, was unveiled in May 1922 by Major General Sir Frederick Maurice and dedicated by the Bishop of Ely. An octagonal shelter, it is constructed principally of oak and has oak seats inside it. A plaque at the entrance reads, "Holy Trinity War Memorial. Passers-by are invited to enter in for rest and shelter". Unfortunately, such shelters, where erected as war memorials, have not always survived the vandalism of recent years, and although this one has not yet met the fate of some in, for example, Leeds or Menston, Yorkshire, where they have been totally destroyed, nevertheless it is very untidy and covered in graffiti and is not at the moment a fitting memorial to the men commemorated.

On a much happier note, the beautiful marble pulpit in the church of St. Anne's in Turton near Bolton, is, in fact, a war memorial to the 60 men of the parish who fell in the First World War. On a nearby pillar is a brass tablet listing the names of the men, while on a similar tablet are the names of the 20 dead of the Second War.

A wreath of poppies rests against the base of the pulpit which is a most impressive and appropriate parish memorial (see Plate C8, p.61).

The Baptist Church of Princes Risborough unveiled in May 1921, a church organ as a memorial to the eight men connected with the church or Sunday School, who had died in the war, and in thanks for the safe return of 58 others.

The unveiling was carried out by Mrs. Lionel de Rothschild, the wife of the M.P. for mid-Bucks., and the service was presided over by the Rev. J. Neighbour. It seems that the organising of the ceremony was not free of anxiety, as the organ arrived to be installed only a couple of days before the day of the unveiling, and the plaque with the names of the 58 men who survived was not completed in time. Moreover, the approximate cost of the organ was £650 and at the time of the unveiling only £308. 19s. 3d. had been raised. By the end of the unveiling and the subsequent service of dedication, however, gifts totalling a further £80 or so had been made and

33
*Newport
Athletic Club
Gates*

confidence was expressed that the organ committee would complete the fund.

The beautiful war memorial in St. John's Church, Derby, to the men of the parish who gave their lives, is one of several made by W. E. Lomas of King Street, Derby, not only for churches but also for towns and villages.

The St. John's memorial consists of lettered panels surrounded by Derbyshire alabaster in a most attractive design (see Plate C6, p.44).

Amongst other church memorials made by Lomas were those for the Victoria Street Chapel, Derby, and for a church in New Basford, Nottinghamshire.

The Parish Church of Almondbury, near Huddersfield, has within it an oak memorial plaque with the names of 110 of the parishioners who died in the Great War. Surmounting the memorial is a bronze crucifix which had been found in the wreckage of Rheims Cathedral after the building had been severely damaged during the war. This crucifix, itself seriously fire-damaged, had been brought back to Almondbury, and in response to a letter from the then Vicar explaining the matter, the Archbishop of Rheims gave his formal consent to the crucifix remaining in Almondbury.

The crucifix has been completely restored and there is no sign now of its earlier condition. As well as the crucifix, there are also on display the framed letters from the Vicar of Almondbury and from the Archbishop of Rheims.

Of the clubs that erected memorials after the war, a large proportion were sports clubs. Birkenhead Park Rugby Union Club dedicated a wooden stand to seat over 1000, as part of the scheme to commemorate its members.

Sixty-seven years later the stand and memorial was demolished because the club could no longer afford to repair damage caused by vandalism, and particularly by two fires in the final year. So, sadly, the stand which was full to capacity for the visits of four All Black touring sides and many other representative matches, no longer exists.

The war memorial gates at the entrance to the grounds of the Newport Athletic Club, in memory of 86 members of the club who fell in the Great War, were unveiled by Lord Tredegar on 6th September, 1923. The names of the dead are inscribed on plaques set into the two stone pillars of the gates.

There are modern additions to the gates of a large sign with the words
NEWPORT ATHLETIC CLUB
raised above the entrance by metal supports from the pillars, and a smaller but even more obtrusive sign fixed to the gate itself and giving directions to the turnstiles and the social club. These signs, particularly the latter, are insensitive and unnecessary and could easily be placed elsewhere. A war memorial cannot be the appropriate place to fix such a direction sign and it is unlikely that many members of the club would think that a better alternative could not be found.

Just inside the boundary fence, near the new East Stand of Scotland's international rugby ground of Murrayfield, is a stone memorial arch. The inscription on it reads —
IN PROUD MEMORY OF THE SCOTTISH RUGBY MEN WHO GAVE THEIR LIVES IN THE GREAT WAR 1914-1918.

Elsewhere in Edinburgh, the clock tower in the Haymarket is to commemorate the players and others associated with the Heart of Midlothian Football Club who fought and fell in the war. Eleven Hearts players joined the forces in 1914 and this started a trend followed by other clubs.

34
*Scottish Rugby
Union
Memorial*

The monument, designed by H. S. Gamley, was unveiled on 9th April, 1922 by Robert Munro, the Secretary for Scotland.

Carved into the stone of the memorial below the level of the clock faces, are the names of the principal battles of the war, on land and at sea.

A memorial tablet on Trent Bridge, Nottingham, commemorates fifty-six members of the city's rowing clubs, who died in the war.

Part of the inscription reads —
THIS MEMORIAL WAS ERECTED BY MEMBERS OF THE NOTTINGHAM ROWING CLUB (N.R.C.), NOTTINGHAM BRITANNIA ROWING CLUB (N.B.R.C.), NOTTINGHAM UNION ROWING CLUB (N.U.R.C.), AND NOTTINGHAM BOAT CLUB (N.B.C.).

An attractive bronze plaque on the wall of the dining room of Halifax Golf Club is inscribed
IN COMMEMORATION OF THE GALLANTRY AND SACRIFICE OF THE MEMBERS OF THIS CLUB WHO FELL IN THE GREAT WAR 1914-1919.

The names of 10 men who died follow, and a further tablet, with 3 names on it, has been erected to the dead of 1939-45.

On the Green at Meriden, the village which is claimed to be at the centre of England, is a Cornish granite obelisk by J. White and Sons of Birmingham. This monument is to the memory of all cyclists killed in the war. The inscription carved in the granite reads,
TO THE LASTING MEMORY OF THOSE CYCLISTS WHO DIED IN THE GREAT WAR 1914-1919,
and the spot has since been the venue for services held by cycling organisations.

Just as the sports clubs which built memorials represented many different sports, so the non-sports clubs covered a full range of interests.

Eldon Lane, near Bishop Auckland in Durham, has a club which, after the war, as the "Eldon Lane & District Workmen's Club & Institute Limited", published a most impressive and comprehensive souvenir booklet entitled

35   *Hearts Memorial, Edinburgh*

24

36 *Halifax Golf Club Memorial*

37 *Meriden Memorial, West Midlands*

What a Club did in the Great War, the Foreword of which is dated November 1919.

  After a short description and history of the club, the book lists its fund-raising and other activities during the war years, describes its own war memorial and the unveiling ceremony, lists the names of the 291 members who served in the war and includes photographs of the 27 who died, gives a description of the activities leading to the

decoration of eight members and prints their photographs, describes the welcome home celebrations and, as a supplement, adds a short history of the war with a list of significant dates and interesting facts and figures.

  The club's own Roll of Honour memorial which was unveiled on 19th July, 1919 is erected inside the main entrance of the club. The names of the dead are in the centre panel and round this list are photographs of each man. Made of oak on a stone base, the memorial is 10ft. 9ins. in height and 5ft. 3ins. in width. The relatives of each of the

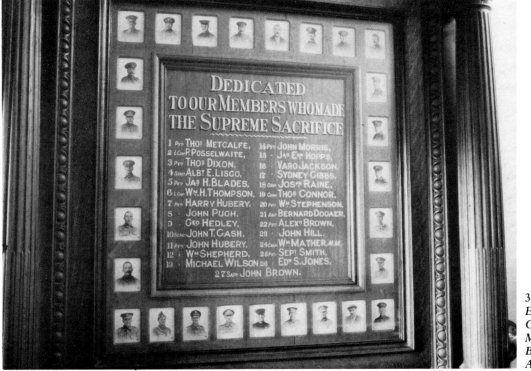

38
*Eldon Lane
Club
Memorial,
Bishop
Auckland*

dead were presented with one large and twelve smaller photographs similar to those on the memorial, the men decorated were each given a present to the value of £5, such as a gold watch, and the others were each presented, at the official Welcome Home Celebrations, with a gold medal bearing his name.

On the main staircase of the Scarborough Conservative Club are three stained glass memorial windows to the dead of the First World War. The central window, with its figure of a saint in armour, has the inscription,

TO THE GLORIOUS MEMORY OF THE MEMBERS OF THE CLUB WHO FELL IN THE GREAT WAR 1914-1918,

while the side windows, with the figures of a soldier and sailor, list 18 members of the club who gave their lives.

The Boys' Brigade movement as a whole sent tens of thousands of its old members into the Services in the Great War.

One service battalion was known as the Boys' Brigade Battalion, the majority of its officers and men being former members of the movement, and other regiments had companies entirely composed of old boys.

Many individuals gained distinction. Nine gained the V.C., 19 the D.S.O., 73 the D.C.M., 79 the M.C., 139 the M.M., 10 the Medaille Militaire, 47 various other awards, Russian and Belgian, and 49 were mentioned in despatches.

The junior members of the Brigade were very active in their support for the war effort, the Newport Battalion, for example, raising sufficient money to purchase and equip two motor ambulances at a cost of nearly £700.

The Newport Battalion, after the war, decided to erect a memorial to their former comrades and this was placed on the stairway of the Town Hall and unveiled on 5th April, 1921. The Roll of Honour, in all 61 names, was read by the officer commanding the Battalion.

The memorial, a mural tablet, was inscribed

IN EVER GRATEFUL MEMORY OF THE OFFICERS AND OLD BOYS OF THE NEWPORT BATTALION OF THE BOYS' BRIGADE WHO GAVE THEIR LIVES IN THE GREAT WAR. A.D. 1914-1919.

The plaque is now housed in the Newport Borough Council Civic Centre, having been carefully preserved after the redevelopment of the area of the former Town Hall.

On the wall of the Great Eastern Hotel, next to Liverpool Street Station, is an ornately decorated plaque with the inscription —

40   *East Anglian Memorial, London*

26

41   *Great Ayton Memorial, North Yorkshire*

THIS MEMORIAL TO THE MEN OF NORFOLK, SUFFOLK, ESSEX AND CAMBRIDGESHIRE WHO FELL IN THE GREAT WAR 1914-1919, IS ERECTED BY THE LONDON SOCIETY OF EAST ANGLIANS.

During the war the Great Eastern Railway station of Liverpool Street was a main staging point for servicemen from East Anglia.

An interesting news item in the *Hampshire Telegraph & Post* of 18th February, 1921, refers to the unveiling of a memorial tablet to nineteen members of the 'Stonehenge Lodge of the Ancient Order of Druids.' The tablet is described as "a humble wooden tablet in black and gold hanging in the lodge room at the Crystal Palace Hotel, Fratton, but its purpose, to perpetuate the memory of those nineteen brethren, will be served none the less."

Of all the categories of memorial, those at places of work varied most in type and scale as, perhaps, might be expected. They ranged from the wall tablet in a small office to the vast monuments of the railway companies.

In the entrance hall to the Council Offices in the High Street, Gosforth, is a bronze memorial plaque to three of the employees of Gosforth Urban District Council who died in action in the First World War.

Thomas James Hudson, a lieutenant in the R.A.F., had been shot down over enemy lines on 20th May, 1917; Robert Irmin, a Lance Corporal in the 5th Northumberland Fusiliers had been killed on the Somme on 20th April, 1917; and John O'Malley, a Private in the 7th Northumberland Fusiliers had been killed at Passchendaele on 26th October, 1917.

The plaque was erected by the officials and workmen of the council "in affectionate remembrance".

In the North Yorkshire village of Great Ayton is a war memorial in the form of a footbridge across a stream, to replace the stepping stones which were previously used.

The bridge is of metal construction and a post at one end supports a plaque inscribed,

THIS BRIDGE WAS PRESENTED BY GEORGE WHITBREAD, UNDER-MANAGER OF AYTON MINES AS A MEMORIAL TO PRIVATE LAWRENCE JOHNSON, PRIVATE ERNEST PEARSON, PRIVATE ROBERT THEOBALD, PRIVATE ARTHUR WILKS, PRIVATE CHARLES WILDMAN, WHO GAVE THEIR LIVES IN THE WAR FOR TRUTH AND JUSTICE. 1914-1919. IT WAS ERECTED BY THEIR FELLOW WORKMEN. JUNE 1919.

In contrast to these memorials to a few men, at the entrance to Euston railway station is the memorial, designed by R. Wynn Owen, to the 3,719 men of the London and North Western Railway Company who died in the Great War. It also now commemorates the dead of 1939-45 who were employees of the London Midland and Scottish Railway, the L.M.S.

The memorial, a stone column on a granite base, with four bronze figures of servicemen at the corners, looks the same today as in a postcard photograph taken after the unveiling on 21st October, 1921, by Field Marshal Earl Haig, but the background is today quite different, a modern office block now dominating the monument.

The memorial to the dead of the Great Eastern Railway Company is situated in the booking hall of Liverpool Street Station. The eleven name-tablets, each listing over a hundred dead, are flanked by classical columns decorated with laurel, and under an appropriate inscription and coat of arms.

To the right of this memorial is a bronze relief portrait above the inscription

TO THE MEMORY OF FIELD MARSHAL SIR HENRY WILSON BART, G.C.B., D.S.O., M.P., WHOSE DEATH OCCURRED ON THURSDAY 22nd JUNE 1922 WITHIN TWO HOURS OF HIS UNVEILING THE ADJOINING MEMORIAL.

Sir Henry Wilson was a Protestant Irishman with a deep hostility to Sinn Fein, and on his

42   *London & North Western Railway Memorial, Euston*

crowd of citizens and were eventually apprehended in Ebury Street despite their being armed, one being felled by a baton thrown by a policeman and the other hit by a bottle thrown by a milkman. They were eventually executed in Wandsworth Prison, and in 1967 their bodies were re-interred in Dublin.

On platform 1, at Paddington Railway Station, is the Great Western Railway Memorial to the dead of the war. The architectural setting is by T. S. Tait and the central bronze figure is by C. S. Jagger.

The figure is of a young soldier, with his greatcoat over his shoulders, and his helmet back on his head, as he reads a letter from home. The statue is on a plinth of granite and against a Cenotaph-shaped background of marble. Beneath it was apparently deposited a lead box, hermetically sealed and placed in a gun-metal casket, specially made at the G.W.R. works at Swindon, and containing the roll of honour with the names of the 2,524 dead of the Great War. The memorial is now to the dead of both wars and an inscription refers to the "3,312 men and women of the Great Western Railway" who "gave their lives for King and Country."

return, after the unveiling ceremony, to his home at the corner of Eaton Place and Belgrave Place, he had been shot and fatally wounded by two I.R.A. men, as he alighted from his cab. The two men, Reginald Dunne and Joseph O'Sullivan, were pursued by police and an ever-increasing

43   *Sir Henry Wilson Memorial, Liverpool Street Station*

44   *Great Western Railway Memorial, Paddington*

28

The soldier figure is a finely executed and impressive work but can easily be overlooked amid the bustle of a busy railway platform. The memorial is, of course, in its original position but it is nevertheless now not seen to its best advantage, if, indeed, it ever was.

The memorial erected by the Midland Railway Company to the memory of 2,833 men of the railway, who gave their lives in the war, was unveiled on Thursday, 15th December, 1921, at 11.45 a.m., by Mr. Charles Booth, the chairman of the company. The memorial stands on Midland Road, Derby, near the railway station.

York, another city with a long railway tradition, has a North Eastern Railway memorial, just inside the city walls and close to the railway station.

This memorial, designed by Sir Edwin Lutyens, has been recently restored, and extended to commemorate the dead of the Second World War. The names of the Great War dead have been re-engraved as the material had weathered badly, and in some places stone has been replaced.

The British Rail Engineers ex-Servicemen's association contributed £8,600 towards the work and British Rail matched the money raised, pound for pound.

The memorial, which was unveiled on 14th June, 1924, by Field Marshal Lord Plumer at a

46   *North Eastern Railway Memorial, York*

ceremony attended by the Archbishop of York, bears the inscription,

IN ABIDING REMEMBRANCE OF THE 2236 MEN OF THE NORTH EASTERN RAILWAY WHO GAVE THEIR LIVES FOR THEIR COUNTRY IN THE GREAT WAR, THE COMPANY PLACES THIS MONUMENT.

The names of the dead are carved into the stone walls of the monument, while those of the 1939–45 war are on slate tablets on the ground between the walls and the Great War Stone.

Elsewhere in York, another company long associated with the city constructed a different type of memorial. Inside the extensive and beautiful grounds of Rowntree Park is an archway with a tablet inscribed,

THIS PARK AND THE ADJOINING PLAYING FIELDS WERE GIVEN TO THE CITY BY ROWNTREE AND CO. LTD. AT THE CLOSE OF THE GREAT WAR (1914-1918) AS A TRIBUTE TO THE MEMORY OF THOSE MEMBERS OF THE COMPANY'S STAFF WHO AT THE COST OF LIFE OR LIMB OR HEALTH, AND IN THE FACE OF INDESCRIBABLE SUFFERING AND HARDSHIP, SERVED THEIR COUNTRY IN HER HOUR OF NEED. MANY WERE INSPIRED BY THE FAITH THAT THIS WAR MIGHT BE THE END OF WAR— THAT VICTORY WOULD LEAD TO AN ENDURING PEACE AND TO GREATER HAPPINESS FOR THE PEOPLES OF THE WORLD.
THE CREATION OF A LEAGUE OF NATIONS WILL BE A FITTING CROWN TO THE FAITH AND HOPE OF THE MEN WHO HAVE FOUGHT AND A TRUE MEMORIAL TO THEIR ENDURANCE, HEROISM, COMRADESHIP AND SACRIFICE".

At the end of the Second World War ornate gates were built at the entrance to the park to commemorate further dead, sad evidence of the fact that sentiments like those expressed on the memorial tablet had gone unheeded (see Plate C7, p.44).

From Port Sunlight and the Lever Brothers companies throughout the world, over 4,000 men fought in the war, and of that number 481 were killed.

Their memorial in the centre of Port Sunlight, now surrounded by alternate displays of red and white roses and in an area of lawns and flower beds, is a cross round the base of which are inscribed the names of the fallen with the dedication

THESE ARE NOT DEAD; SUCH SPIRITS NEVER DIE.

Encircling the foot of the cross a group of bronze sculptured figures symbolises the defence of the home. One soldier stands with fixed bayonet, another kneels to fire and a third, wounded, is about to receive aid from a nurse, while children look on in alarm. The platform supporting the cross is surrounded by a low parapet and at intervals are further bronze groups representing the sea, land and air forces and the Red Cross. Finally, there are figures of children offering garlands in gratitude for the sacrifice made.

The designer of this beautiful and impressive memorial, was the sculptor Sir W. Goscombe John R. A. who was well served by granite masons Messrs. William Kirkpatrick Limited of Manchester and by the bronze founder Mr. A. B. Burton of Thames Ditton.

The unveiling on 3rd December, 1921, was by ex-Sergeant T. G. Eames who was a former employee of the Company and who had been blinded at the Somme. He was guided and assisted by ex-Private R. E. Cruikshank who was awarded the V.C. in 1918 for his actions in Palestine.

As well as the names on the memorial, the names of all who served and their war records are commemorated both by a book deposited in a cavity in the memorial and by one placed in Christ Church, Port Sunlight, by the Hon. W. Hulme Lever.

At a meeting of the staff of the Bank of England on 18th February, 1919, when the Chief Cashier, Mr. (later Sir) Ernest Harvey, was in the chair, it was resolved that a War Memorial Scheme should be undertaken and eventually this took a three-part form. Firstly, a Memorial Service, secondly, the endowment of a hospital

47
Port Sunlight Memorial, Cheshire

30

48   *Bank of England Memorial
(Photo by kind permission of the
Bank of England)*

On the base of the statue is the inscription,
TO THE COMRADES WHO AT DUTY'S CALL CROSSED
THE DARK WATERS TO THE FURTHER SHORE —
1914-1919.

The memorial was unveiled on Armistice
Day 1921 by the Governor (by then, Montagu
Norman) and dedicated by the Archdeacon of
London, the Venerable E. E. Holmes.

Inside the bank building there is also a
memorial listing those employees who served
during the war.

A bronze plaque on a wall inside the
entrance porch to the City of London's
Guildhall, represents the war memorial to the
Members of the Corporation, their sons, and the
Officers of the Corporation.

The plaque, dedicated on Thursday, January
20th, 1921, after a service in the Church of St.
Lawrence Jewry, bears the names of one
Member, 33 sons of Members and 78 Officers.

The order of the procession from the church
to the Guildhall was, firstly the choir, then the
Members of the General Council, the City Lands
Committee, the Under-Sheriffs, the City
Officers, representatives of the Army, the
Aldermen, the Sheriffs, the Lord Mayor escorted
by the Rector of St. Lawrence Jewry, and finally
the relatives of the fallen.

The Parliamentary War Memorial is situated
at the top of the steps at the south end of
Westminster Hall and near the St. Stephen's
entrance to the House of Commons. This is
unfortunately now a security area and because of
these arrangements it is no longer possible to
stand back and look at the memorial from any
distance, as the designer, Sir Bertram MacKennal
must have assumed would be likely.

The Prince of Wales unveiled the memorial
on Wednesday, 22nd November, 1922. A Gothic
Screen, it has at its centre a winged figure holding
a scroll, and to the right and left of the figure are
panels inscribed with the names of those who fell
in the war, including that of Raymond Asquith,
the Prime Minister's son. The dedication
inscribed on the base of the central figure is as
follows —
TO THE MEMBERS AND OFFICERS OF BOTH HOUSES OF
PARLIAMENT AND SONS OF MEMBERS AND OFFICERS
OF THE HOUSE OF COMMONS WHO IN THE GREAT WAR
CONSUMMATED WITH THEIR LIVES THE TRADITIONS
OF PUBLIC SERVICE IN THE CAUSE OF RIGHT AND
LIBERTY, THIS MEMORIAL IS DEDICATED IN HOMAGE
AND AFFECTION.

The sons of peers and the sons of officers of
the House of Lords, are commemorated in the
Royal Gallery.

Also inscribed on the memorial is an extract
from the XIV Philippic of Cicero
commemorating the death in battle of the
Consuls, Hirtius and Pansa, in BC43. The
translation of the Latin is —
"Happy was your death. You paid for your
fatherland the common debt that all men owe
to nature, So this fabric is reared, and the letters
inscribed upon it, as eternal testimonies of
your valour. Those who look upon your
monument will never cease to tell of your
deeds in words of gratitude. And so instead of
the mortality of human life you have obtained
immortality."

bed, and thirdly, a memorial in the Bank garden.
The Memorial Service was held in Southwark
Cathedral on Saturday, 12th April, 1919, in the
presence of a crowded congregation including
the Governor of the Bank, Sir Brien Cokayne.
The names of the fallen were read aloud from the
steps of the altar.

Two months later, a bed was endowed in the
Astley Cooper ward of Guy's Hospital.

Finally, a sculptor was appointed, Mr.
Richard R. Goulden, formerly a captain in the
Royal Engineers, and his design for a memorial,
in the form of St. Christopher and the Holy
Child, was accepted. The garden, which was
re-laid to receive the memorial, had once been
the churchyard of St. Christopher-le-Stocks.

The bronze life-size figure of St.
Christopher, with the child on his shoulder, is
mounted on a pedestal of Portland stone bearing,
on three sides, bronze tablets on which are the
names of the 71 employees of the Bank who gave
their lives. Inset on the front of the pedestal is a
bronze cross.

A Lloyd's Memorial Book contains photographs of the men who fell in the war, together with their regiment and rank, and some information about their death. The book commemorates 31 Members of Lloyd's, 5 Annual Subscribers, 1 Associate, and 179 Substitutes and Representatives.

The book also contains a photograph of the Lloyd's War Memorial which, since the construction of the new and controversial building, does not yet seem to have been re-sited. If it has, then Lloyd's security and information services appear to have no knowledge of the fact, nor, indeed, any great interest in the matter.

The Stock Exchange has as its war memorial a large marble tablet and a Roll of Honour with the names of the fallen, in a prominent position inside the building's entrance.

There is also a Memorial Book printed in 1920, and listing the Members and Clerks who fell in the war. Photographs and brief biographies of each man are provided with more information being given than in the similar Lloyd's book.

For example, Captain Robert Bingley Herbert of the London Regiment was born in 1882 and became a member of the Stock Exchange in 1907 when he joined the firm founded by his grandfather, G. S. Herbert & Sons.

He was killed at Loos on 30th September, 1915, and the entry goes on, "The men of his section have placed an *In Memoriam* notice in *The Times* every year on the anniversary of his death, in these terms: 'In loyal and loving memory of our gallant officer, Captain R. B. Herbert. His Boys'."

Another remarkable entry concerns Lieutenant Henry Webber. Born in 1849 and educated at Tonbridge and Pembroke College, Oxford, he was a well-known sportsman and prominent member of the Surrey Stag Hunt, a good shot and a keen cricketer. He often captained an M.C.C. side against his old school and when he was 55 scored over 200 runs in a club match. He was also a J.P., a member of the Surrey County Council, honorary treasurer of the local cottage hospital, and for many years a church warden of his parish. He entered the Stock Exchange in 1872 and became a member of his father-in-law's firm Norman Morris & Co.

At the outbreak of war, despite his age, he tried several times to join the army in virtually any capacity but was rejected by the War Office. Nevertheless he persevered, and was within a few weeks of his 68th birthday when he was at length gazetted on 1st May, 1916, to the South Lancashire Regiment. With his knowledge of horses he was appointed Transport Officer of the 7th Battalion and took part in the opening phases of the Battle of the Somme, including the capture of La Boiselle on 3rd July, 1916.

A fortnight later he wrote to his old school, "Fifty years ago I got my colours in the XI and fifty-one years ago I was bowling versus the Old Boys and looking at some of them as "sitters", and in the "sere and yellow leaf". And here I am, Lieutenant in H.M. Army having to salute three sons if I meet them out here, a colonel and two majors".

Four days later, before his letter was received, he was already dead, struck on the head by a fragment of shell while at Battalion H.Q. in Mametz Wood. He was buried in a military cemetery south of Albert, and his commanding officer wrote, "He was so gallant and full of energy. We all had the greatest admiration and respect for him."

Special messages of sympathy were received by his family from the King and Queen, and from the Army Council, and he was mentioned in despatches by Sir Douglas Haig.

49   *The Parliamentary War Memorial*

Chapter IV

Military Memorials

If, under the heading of "Military", we include the memorials of all three services, army, navy and air force, and if we consider corps, regimental and even battalion memorials, then the scope is enormous and there are some magnificent monuments to examine, particularly in London.

One of the most impressive of all war memorials is that erected in 1925, at Hyde Park Corner, to the 49,076 dead of the Royal Artillery. It was designed by Adams, Holden and Pearson, the sculptor being Charles Sargeant Jagger.

A massive stone structure, the memorial is surmounted by an enormous howitzer in stone, and it is said that the gun's elevation and position is such that a shell from it, if it could be given sufficient charge, would land on the Somme.

On the sides of the monument are marvellous bronze figures of artillerymen, and stone reliefs of artillery in action.

At one end is the bronze figure of a dead soldier covered with his greatcoat and with his helmet placed on his chest. Around the figure are inscribed the words

HERE WAS A ROYAL FELLOWSHIP OF DEATH

and on the stone below,

BENEATH THIS STONE IS BURIED THE ROLL OF HONOUR OF THOSE WHOSE MEMORY IS PERPETUATED BY THIS MEMORIAL. THEY WILL RETURN NEVER MORE, BUT THEIR GLORY WILL ABIDE FOR EVER.

51   *The Royal Artillery Memorial, detail*

50
The Royal Artillery Memorial, Hyde Park Corner

52   *The Royal Artillery Memorial, detail*

Close to the Artillery Memorial, the Machine Gun Corps Memorial erected in 1925 at Hyde Park Corner, has as its main feature a bronze figure of David by Derwent Wood. David is holding the slain Goliath's sword, and an inscription on the base of the memorial is

SAUL HATH SLAIN HIS THOUSANDS BUT DAVID HIS TENS OF THOUSANDS,

perhaps a strange choice of quotation.

To either side of the figure and at a slightly lower level, is a bronze machine gun covered by two laurel wreaths, and on the back of the central pedestal is inscribed a short history of the Corps. Its Colonel-in-Chief was King George V and it was formed on 14th October, 1915, and disbanded on 15th July, 1922. During the war 1,120 officers and 12,671 other ranks were killed, and 2,881 officers and 45,377 other ranks were wounded, missing or prisoners of war.

The Cavalry Memorial in Hyde Park, not far from Hyde Park Corner, has a magnificent bronze by Adrian Jones, of a mounted St. George, with sword aloft, triumphing over the dragon. The figure is on a stone plinth with a bronze frieze depicting imperial cavalry, and the inscription on the plinth reads,

ERECTED BY THE CAVALRY OF THE EMPIRE IN MEMORY OF COMRADES WHO GAVE THEIR LIVES IN THE WAR 1914-1919.

The memorial has a granite base, and there is a wall of the same material behind the central figure. On this wall, on bronze plates, are listed the various cavalry regiments of the Empire, from Britain, India, Australia, Canada, New Zealand and South Africa. Also on the tablets are the names French, Haig, Allenby and Robertson, and it was the first named, Field Marshal Lord Ypres, who unveiled the memorial on 22nd May, 1924 on its original site at Stanhope Gate.

The bronzes by Gilbert Ledward are the most striking feature of the Guards Division Memorial designed by H. C. Bradshaw and erected in 1926 on the St. James Park side of Horse Guards Parade. The stone monolith is itself elegant and impressive but attention is instantly focused on the figures of five life-sized guardsmen, each from a different guards regiment, standing in line and facing the parade ground.

Bronze panels are set into the other three sides of the monument, the scene of artillery in

53   *The Machine Gun Corps Memorial,*
      Hyde Park Corner

action, on the side facing St. James Park, being
particularly interesting.

Later in the 20's Ledward was appointed
Professor of Sculpture at the Royal College of
Art.

In the Victoria Embankment Gardens in
London is the 1920 Camel Corps Memorial. A
bronze figure of a soldier mounted on a camel,
stands on a stone pedestal on the sides of which
are two bronze relief plaques and two bronze
name tablets. An inscription reads

TO THE GLORIOUS AND IMMORTAL MEMORY OF THE
OFFICERS, N.C.O.'s AND MEN OF THE IMPERIAL CAMEL
CORPS, BRITISH, AUSTRALIAN, NEW ZEALAND AND
INDIAN, WHO FELL IN ACTION OR DIED OF WOUNDS
AND DISEASE IN EGYPT, SINAI AND PALESTINE
1916-17-18.

54   *The Cavalry Memorial, Hyde Park*

55   *The Cavalry Memorial on its original site*

35

The memorial's sculptor was Cecil Brown, and the bronzes were cast, as were so many at that time, by Burton of Thames Ditton.

The Royal Air Force Memorial on the Embankment at Whitehall Stairs was designed by Sir Reginald Blomfield and is surmounted by a sculptured gilt eagle by Sir William Reid Dick. The eagle looks across the Thames, but the main inscription is on the Embankment side of the memorial.

IN MEMORY OF ALL RANKS OF THE ROYAL NAVAL AIR SERVICE, ROYAL FLYING CORPS, ROYAL AIR FORCE AND THOSE AIR FORCES FROM EVERY PART OF THE BRITISH EMPIRE, WHO GAVE THEIR LIVES IN WINNING VICTORY FOR THEIR KING AND COUNTRY 1914-18. I BARE YOU ON EAGLES WINGS AND BROUGHT YOU UNTO MYSELF.

The monument was unveiled on 16th July, 1923, by the Prince of Wales. Amongst others who attended the ceremony were the Duke of York, Air Chief Marshal Sir Hugh Trenchard, Lord Beatty, and the air attachés of France, Belgium and the U.S.A.

At the side entrance to the crypt of St. Martin's-in-the-Field, Trafalgar Square, is a tribute to the Old Contemptibles of the Great War.

At the bottom of a flight of stairs and to the side of the entrance, the memorial is an arch of black marble with wrought iron gates painted mainly black but with gold decorations.

An inscription reads

MONS TO YPRES 1914.

56   *The Guards Memorial*

57   *The Guards Memorial*

58   *The Guards Memorial*

59   *The Camel Corps Memorial*

60   *The R.A.F. Memorial*

61   *"Old Contemptibles" Memorial*

Also carved in the stone are the battle honours of

MONS, MARNE, AISNE, AND YPRES.

Also in St. Martin's is the memorial to the men of the 14th, 15th and 16th battalions of the Royal Warwickshire Regiment, which was unveiled on 12th November, 1933. This work, similar in style to the Cenotaph in Whitehall, was designed by A. E. Lucas, a member of the 16th battalion, and made by the firm of J. White & Sons, the Birmingham stonemasons who made so many local war memorials.

The monument features a bronze Antelope and is guarded by three bronze columns, each bearing an original cap badge, and a stout silk cord in regimental colours.

Many other regimental memorials are to be found in the principal churches or cathedrals of the county towns or main cities.

Guildford had long been the depot of the Queen's Regiment, and the Regimental Chapel is in Holy Trinity Church, Guildford.

In the church in June 1919 a solemn memorial service was held for the 8,000 men of all ranks of the Queen's who fell in the war, and at the close of the service the colours of the regiment were crowned with laurel wreaths by the Lord Lieutenant, Lord Ashcombe.

Two years later, on 4th June, 1921, another huge congregation was present at the service of unveiling and dedication of the Queen's war memorial in the church. General Sir Charles Monro carried out the unveiling and the Bishop of Winchester, Dr. E. S. Talbot, offered the dedication.

Over £3,000 had been subscribed, and the memorial itself had been designed by a former officer of the regiment, Captain Stanley Hall. His design provided for a central niche on the north wall of Holy Trinity Church, to hold a bronze and

Another memorial to the same body of men is in St. Martin's Parish Church, Birmingham, in the form of a stone wall tablet put up by the Birmingham branch of the Old Contemptibles Association.

The inscription reads,

TO THE GLORY OF GOD AND IN MEMORY OF GENERAL FRENCH'S CONTEMPTIBLE LITTLE ARMY.

62
The Queen's Regiment Memorial, Guildford

63
The Devonshire Regiment Memorial, Exeter

glass casket containing a book inscribed with the names of the dead. Above the niche was the regimental badge, the Paschal Lamb, and on either side were carved oak Corinthian columns and panels with the regiment's battle honours. Also on each side was oak panelling 36ft. long and over 11ft. high.

Above the memorial were placed three stained glass windows, subscribed for by the 3rd, 8th and 10th Battalions.

In St. Chad's Church, Shrewsbury, is a simple plaque commemorating 4,700 men of the King's Shropshire Light Infantry who fell in the Great War.

There are several regimental memorials of the First World War in Canterbury Cathedral.

There is one to the dead of the 16th The Queen's Lancers with a Book of Remembrance in the niche below the memorial, and one to the Carabiniers with a bronze figure of a dead soldier covered by a flag, again with a Book of Remembrance set in the wall below.

Within the Cathedral is the chapel of the Royal East Kent Regiment, "The Buffs" (see Plate C9, p.61).

The memorial to the men of the Devonshire Regiment who lost their lives in the 1914–18 war is in Exeter Cathedral. A most realistic figure in bronze, it depicts a soldier of the regiment in action, kneeling with bayonet fixed and one elbow resting on the sandbag in front of him, while in the background, in the ruins of a village, can be seen a crucifix still standing.

Unfortunately, the area of the cathedral close to the memorial seems to be used on occasions for stacking folding chairs. This seems unnecessary and inappropriate, and is surely something that can be avoided if a little thought is given to the problem.

The regimental chapel of the Durham Light Infantry was dedicated by the Lord Bishop of Durham on 20th October, 1923, two smaller pre-Reformation chapels in the South Transept of Durham Cathedral having been assigned for this purpose the previous year. At first the chapel was established as a memorial to those who gave

64
The Durham Light Infantry Memorial

39

their lives in the 1914–18 war, but since the amalgamation of the regiment with other light infantry county regiments in the late 1960's, the chapel has been dedicated also to the regiment itself which is no longer in being.

Within the chapel a lectern holds Books of Remembrance for each World War, pages of each book being turned daily. The names commemorated in the books number 12,606 for 1914–18 and 3,011 for 1939–45.

Another interesting feature is a wooden cross which commemorates the men of the 6th, 8th and 9th battalions who fell in an attack on the Butte de Warlencourt on the Somme on the 5th and 6th November, 1916. The cross was made of scrap wood and ration boxes and erected on the Butte the next day. It remained there until 1926 when it was brought home to the chapel.

Inside Chester Cathedral is a Roll of Honour as a memorial to the dead of H.M.S. *Chester* at the Battle of Jutland, and a framed photograph of the vessel itself. Amongst the men's names is that of John Travers Cornwall, 16 years old, who received the V.C. for his actions during the battle when, although mortally wounded, he stayed alone at his exposed post.

In early 1920 a faculty was granted by the church authorities for the necessary alteration to the south transept of Beverley Minster, in order to form an East Yorkshire Regiment war memorial.

This was to consist of six lancet windows of stained glass, and the formation of a soldiers' chapel within which would be a shrine recording the names of the men of the regiment who fell in the war.

The scheme finally came to fruition on 16th June, 1921, with the unveiling of the windows and shrine by the Lord Lieutenant of the County, Lord Nunburnholme, and the Colonel of the Regiment, Major–General Inglefield, and the subsequent dedication by the Archbishop of York.

The windows, with scenes illustrating the age-long conflict between good and evil, were

66   *The King's Royal Rifle Corps Memorial, Winchester*

designed by Dunston J. Powell of the Birmingham firm, Messrs. Hardman. Messrs. Elwell of Beverley were responsible for the richly-carved oak mouldings of the screens of the chapel, and Mr. Davidson of London for the shrine. The names recorded in the shrine eventually totalled some 7,500 of the East Yorkshire Regiment, and also about 7,000 East Yorkshire men who served in other units, making the memorial a joint regimental and county one.

In York Minster, the chapel of the King's Own Yorkshire Light Infantry contains a commemorative plaque to the 9,447 men of the regiment who fell in the war, and also Books of Remembrance for the dead of both World Wars. There is also a separate memorial to the 6th Battalion K.O.Y.L.I., with a bronze figure of a soldier-saint and a list of the battalion's battle honours from 1914 to 1918.

The First World War memorial of the King's Royal Rifle Corps stands in the Cathedral Close at Winchester. A stone monument surmounted by the bronze figure of a rifleman standing at ease, it is in memory of the 567 officers and 12,257 other ranks killed, and of approximately 145,000 injured.

The Hampshire County Memorial in the Cathedral Close at Winchester is a stone cross on a high plinth close to the doors of the Cathedral, and 100 yards from the memorial of the King's Royal Rifle Corps. Amongst other inscriptions on the monument there is one to 7,541 men of the Hampshire Regiment who died in the war, one to 737 men of H.M.S. *Hampshire* sunk by a mine off the Orkneys on 5th June, 1916, with Lord Kitchener aboard, and one to 460 citizens of Winchester "who upheld under King George V the traditions of service and sacrifice handed down from the days of King Alfred."

At the base of the cross on four sides are the arms of Hampshire, the Isle of Wight, the City of Winchester and the Hampshire Regiment. The architect, Herbert Baker, while in Ypres with the War Graves Commission, arranged for a stone from the ruined Cloth Hall to be sent to Winchester and this was let into the pavement below the Hampshire Regiments' inscription.

The memorial was unveiled on Monday, 31st October, 1921, by the Lord Lieutenant of the County, Major-General Seely. Amongst those attending the ceremony were the Duke of Wellington and Lord Montague of Beaulieu.

Another tribute to the Hampshires is at Fampoux Gardens in Charminster, Bournemouth, which were constructed by unemployed ex-servicemen as a memorial to the stand by the Regiment at Fampoux in the Battle of Arras in March 1918. The Corporation supplied the land and tools and equipment, and financial support came from the local British Legion and the Rotary Club. The garden was officially opened on 21st April, 1923, by Major-General Brooking and is still there today, well-tended and peaceful and with an appropriately inscribed plaque set in a block of stone.

Further along the South Coast, at

67   *The Royal Navy Memorial, Portsmouth*

Portsmouth, is one of three Naval War Memorials designed by Sir Robert Lorimer.

During the war, the Royal Navy and the navies of the Dominions lost some 48,000 men of whom no fewer than 25,563 were lost or buried at sea and were not recorded in any cemetery or on any battlefield.

In 1920 the Admiralty appointed a Committee to report on the most suitable form and position for a memorial to these men, and as a result of its recommendations three identical monuments were erected at the three home ports which were the manning ports of the Royal Navy; at Plymouth on the Hoe, at Portsmouth on Southsea Common and at Chatham at the "Great Lines".

Each memorial is in the form of an obelisk supported at the four corners by buttresses and each buttress carries a sculptured figure of a lion couchant, looking outwards.

On the base and the buttresses are bronze panels bearing the names of the dead who belonged to the port in question, and on the four faces of the memorial are large bronze panels listing the general actions at sea, Heligoland, Coronel, Falkland Islands, Dogger Bank and Jutland; single ship actions; actions with enemy land forces; and, on the fourth face, the inscription

IN HONOUR OF THE NAVY AND TO THE ABIDING MEMORY OF THOSE RANKS AND RATINGS OF THIS PORT WHO LAID DOWN THEIR LIVES IN THE DEFENCE OF THE EMPIRE AND HAVE NO KNOWN GRAVE THAN THE SEA, 1914-18.

41

Above the base, a column of Portland stone about 100ft. high is crowned by a large copper sphere supported by figures representing the four winds. About a third of the way up the column is carved the badge of the Royal Navy and near the top the prows of four ships are carved in stone.

The memorials were much enlarged after the Second World War to accommodate the names of those lost between 1939 and 1945.

That at Southsea Common, to over 9,700 men of the Portsmouth Port Division who were lost at sea, was the last of the three to be unveiled, the Duke of York performing the ceremony on Wednesday, 15th October, 1924. The naval authorities provided accommodation for 10,000 ticket holders to attend the unveiling but, in all, a crowd of easily three times that number was drawn to the spot.

The memorial at Plymouth, to over 7,000 men, is on the north side of the famous Hoe, between the Armada Memorial and the Drake Statue. It was unveiled on 29th July, 1924, by Prince George again in the presence of a vast crowd of some 25,000.

68   *The Sherwood Foresters Memorial, Crich Hill*

Also on the Hoe a few hundred yards from the Naval Memorial and the Armada Memorial is that erected by the Plymouth Division of the Royal Marines. Surmounted by a bronze winged figure slaying a German eagle, the pedestal has at its base two stone figures in army and naval uniforms respectively.

To return to regimental memorials, the Sherwood Foresters' War Memorial is a 63ft. high tower built on Crich Hill, Derbyshire, 955ft. above sea level.

Designed by Lt. Colonel A. W. Brewill who commanded the "Robin Hood" Battalion of the regiment during the war, the tower was built by Mr. Joseph Payne of Crich.

On the headstone above the door was inscribed
TO THE MEMORY OF THE 11,409 MEN OF ALL RANKS OF THE SHERWOOD FORESTERS (NOTTS. & DERBY REGT.) WHO GAVE THEIR LIVES FOR THEIR KING AND COUNTRY IN THE GREAT WAR 1914-1919, AND IN HONOUR OF 140,000 OF THEIR COMRADES WHO SERVED DURING THE WAR IN THIRTY-TWO BATTALIONS OF THE REGIMENT, THIS MONUMENT IS GRATEFULLY ERECTED BY THE PEOPLE OF THE COUNTIES OF NOTTINGHAM AND DERBY.
TO REMIND US OF THEIR SACRIFICE AND OUR DUTY.

Above the inscription was placed a bronze laurel wreath and in the front of the tower above the doorway is the regimental badge in bronze, and a stone cross to which is affixed a bronze sword.

Inside the tower 58 steps lead to a landing from which there is a view of seven counties, and in which is mounted a light to be lit on anniversaries of the regiment's battles.

The memorial was opened on 6th August, 1923, by General Sir Horace L. Smith-Dorrien, Colonel of the Regiment, in the presence of 50,000 people, and an annual pilgrimage to the hill is still held.

A monument to Smith-Dorrien was later built on the approach to the tower.

The War Memorial to the Leicestershire Yeomanry is also on high ground, in Bradgate Park, north of Leicester. On a clear day the view from "Old John" extends over many miles and the column of the memorial commands that view.

On a plaque on the face of the monument are the words —
TO THE GLORY OF GOD AND IN MEMORY OF THOSE GALLANT LEICESTERSHIRE YEOMEN WHO FELL IN THE GREAT WAR 1914-1918.
and on another plaque are the battle honours of the Yeomanry from the Boer War up to the "Pursuit to Mons" in 1918.

A Second World War tablet has subsequently been added.

At Kempston, near Bedford, is the tribute to the 336 officers and 5,745 other ranks of the Bedfordshire Regiment who fell in the First World War. This attractive roadside memorial which also now commemorates the Second World War, has as a background a Garden of Remembrance.

The memorial to the York and Lancaster Regiment is on a beautiful site in Weston Park, Sheffield, between the University and the Mappin Art Gallery.

C1   *Haig, Whitehall*

C2   *The Huntriss Memorial*

C3   *The Mobbs Memorial*

C4   *Uppingham School Memorial Chapel*

C5 *Magdalene College Memorial*

C6 *St. John's, Derby*

C7 *Rowntree Park*

44

69   *The Bedfordshire Regiment Memorial, Kempston*

This striking monument to the 8,814 officers and men of the regiment who fell in the First World War, has a tall granite column surmounted by a bronze winged figure of Victory, and supported at its base by the bronze figures of an officer, with drawn revolver, and of a private, with sleeves rolled up and with rifle and helmet slung over his shoulder. Carved into the granite is the regimental badge and at the front and rear are sculptured impedimenta of war, weapons, helmet, greatcoat, drum, ammunition box, flag and so on.

Behind the memorial are two trees with a plaque inscribed,

PLANTED BY MEMBERS OF THE 2/3 WEST RIDING FIELD AMBULANCE OLD COMRADES ASSOCIATION IN MEMORY OF THEIR FALLEN COMRADES 1914-1918.

The Green Howards' memorial stands at the top of a flight of steps at the end of Frenchgate, Richmond, North Yorkshire. A photograph taken of the dedication ceremony in the early 1920's shows the view from Frenchgate, but the more common view is from the main road at the higher level, and from there, unfortunately, the memorial looks less impressive, standing as it does at pavement level.

From Frenchgate it is a most attractive monument, with its Celtic Cross made from stone obtained from the Aske Estate and presented to the regiment by Lord Zetland. Stone was obtained from the same source when the 1939-1945 dates were later added.

On the memorial are the badge of the regiment, at the time of the war without the words "Green Howards", and the inscription,

TO COMMEMORATE THE GALLANT DEAD OF THE YORKSHIRE REGIMENT, THE GREEN HOWARDS, WHO FOUGHT AND DIED FOR THEIR COUNTRY IN THE GREAT WAR AND WHOSE NAMES ARE RECORDED IN A BOOK PLACED IN THE RICHMOND PARISH CHURCH.

Close to the Church of St. Thomas the Martyr, in the centre of Newcastle, stands the memorial designed by Sir William Goscombe John, and unveiled by the Prince of Wales in 1923, which was a gift to the city from Sir George and Lady Renwick, to commemorate certain battalions of the Northumberland Fusiliers. The granite monument and base have a large group of bronze figures on one side, and three sculptured figures in granite on the other. The bronze group on the memorial, named "The Response", shows Tyneside men in the "rush to the Colours" which typified the early weeks of the war.

70 *The York & Lancaster Regiment Memorial, Sheffield*

71   *The Green Howards Memorial, Richmond*

Northumberland Fusiliers, accompanied by two drummer boys, head the procession and they

are followed by other men, carrying tools or rifles, in uniform or in working clothes, some saying goodbye to their families, others waving enthusiastically. Above them, flags fly and a winged figure sounds a trumpet. The whole scene is both moving and inspiring, and there are many small episodes, such as a boy carrying his father's kit-bag, and a workman hugging his wife and baby, which must have seemed unbearably poignant to many of those seeing them for the first time, a few years after the end of the war.

The bronze group is 23ft. long and about 7ft. high, rising to 12ft. to the top of the trumpeting figure. On the base of the pedestal are the words NON SIBI SED PATRIAE (Not for himself but for his country).

On the back of the memorial are figures of St. George flanked by a Northumberland Fusilier in the uniform of the Great War, and by a soldier in the uniform of 1674, the year in which the regiment was enrolled. An inscription reads,

TO COMMEMORATE THE RAISING OF THE B COMPANY 9th BATTALION AND THE 16th, 18th AND 19th SERVICE BATTALIONS, NORTHUMBERLAND FUSILIERS, BY THE NEWCASTLE AND GATESHEAD CHAMBER OF COMMERCE AUGUST — OCTOBER 1914.

The gateway of Glencorse Barracks, on the main Edinburgh Road near Penecuik, is a war memorial to the First World War dead of the Royal Scots. Two stone gate-houses frame the gates themselves, on which are badges of the regiment.

The superb bronze group of the Cameronians' memorial near the Art Gallery in Kelvingrove Park, Glasgow, would perhaps not appeal to those who prefer such memorials to be

72   *The Northumberland Fusiliers — "The Response"*

73   *A detail from "The Response"*

pacific or compromising in nature. Between a machine gunner and a fallen comrade an infantryman charges forward, his face set with determination and the effect is an uncomplicated tribute to the basic military virtues of courage and self-sacrifice.

The sculptor of this 1924 work was P. Lindsey Clark and on the stone base is the following inscription,

TO THE GLORIOUS MEMORY OF ALL RANKS THE CAMERONIANS (SCOTTISH RIFLES) WHO, TO UPHOLD LIBERTY AND JUSTICE IN THE WORLD, LAID DOWN THEIR LIVES IN THE TWO WORLD WARS.

Also inscribed are the lines

O VALIANT HEARTS, WHO TO YOUR GLORY CAME THROUGH DUST OF CONFLICT AND THRO' BATTLE FLAME, TRANQUIL YOU LIE, YOUR KNIGHTLY VIRTUE PROVED, YOUR MEMORY HALLOWED IN THE LAND YOU LOVED.

One Scottish memorial which does not strictly come within the bounds of this book since it is situated abroad, is that of Aberdeen granite made after the Great War for Beaumont Hamel in France, to commemorate the 51st Highland Division who fought there during the Battle of the Somme.

One soldier who fought with the 4th Battalion Gordon Highlanders, 51st Highland Division, and was wounded at Beaumont Hamel, took his young son after the war to a granite yard in Aberdeen (Garden & Co., Victoria Granite Works, King Street) to see the work before it was sent to be erected on the battlefield.

Less than twenty years later that youngster, J. Stewart, by then himself in the 4th Battalion Gordon Highlanders, visited the same memorial at Beaumont Hamel whilst in France with the British Expeditionary Force before Dunkirk.

74   *A detail from "The Response"*

47

75   *The Royal Scots Memorial, Glencorse Barracks, Penecuik*

The dead of the 51st Highland Division were, of course, also commemorated by the memorials of their own regiments, and this sort of duplication was common.

A similar example is to be found in the memorial at the Royal Military College at Sandhurst to the former cadets who died. Their names are inscribed on the many pillars of the chapel, and are grouped together firstly by regiment, and then in order of the year of their death.

76   *The Cameronians Memorial, Glasgow*

Chapter V

Villages

It is by an examination of village war memorials that the dreadful impact of the First World War can perhaps most readily be understood. To read a long list of names on a village green memorial, in the centre of a hamlet which seems to have a mere handful of houses, is to realize how drastically and permanently communities were affected, particularly those as closely knit as the average village.

Memorials in larger towns and cities, because of the number of dead, were normally unable to list the names, which were often recorded elsewhere in Books of Remembrance. Therefore, although the scale of the monuments in large towns is normally more impressive, the seemingly disproportionately long lists of the names of the fallen, often with many apparently from the same family, which are common in villages, can be more revealing and moving.

The commonest form of village memorial is the cross, normally in the centre, for example on the village green if one exists, but also frequently to be found in the churchyard.

The war memorial cross in the village of Addington, near Croydon, was unusual in that, despite the size of the community, it was dedicated by the Archbishop of Canterbury, Dr. Davidson.

It was not, however, the first memorial cross that he had dedicated in the village. The Archbishops of Canterbury once used Addington Palace as a country home, and five 19th century Archbishops are buried in the church or churchyard, and to these Dr. Davidson had dedicated a memorial in May 1911. The two crosses are within about twenty yards of each other, and a photograph of the war memorial shows the earlier cross quite clearly in the background, just inside the wall of the churchyard.

The tribute to the 22 men of Addington who died in the war, is on a corner site and takes the form of a Celtic cross in silver-grey granite, with a carved double-handed Crusader's sword on its face.

It was dedicated by the Primate on 25th March, 1922, after having been unveiled by Lieutenant Colonel Arthur Goschen D.S.O., the name of whose brother, Christopher Goschen, appears on the monument.

77   *The Addington Memorial, near Croydon*

In the small village of Chaddleworth, near Newbury, the dead of the First World War are commemorated by a stone Celtic Cross in a beautifully kept plot in the centre of the village. Amongst the sixteen names inscribed on the memorial are those of three Pearce brothers, Jack, Tom and Douglas. Jack, however, was not killed in the war. Now a sprightly 95 year old he still lives in the village, with his wife Ida, aged 92,

see to it that their names
Be Not Forgotten.

W.J.BRADLEY. LCE.CPL. ROYAL BERKS. REG
H.CHISMAN. CPL. BERKS. YEOMANRY.
W.GOATLEY. PTE. ROYAL BERKS. REGT.
H.LEWINGTON. PTE. ROYAL BERKS. REGT
A.PEARCE & D.PEARCE PTES. ROYAL BERKS. R
J.PEARCE SERGT. HANTS. REGT.
E.POUNDS. PTE. ROYAL BERKS. REGT.
J.POWELL. PTE. ROYAL BERKS REGT.
W.PULLINGER. LCE.CPL. ROYAL BERKS REG
S.SAYERS. PTE. ROYAL BERKS. REGT
A.SMITH & G.SMITH. PTES ROYAL BERKS RE
W.J.UZZELL. DRIVER ROYAL GARRISON ART
A.WITHERS. SAPPER ROYAL ENGINEERS.
P.H.N.WROUGHTON. MAJOR BERKS. YEOMAN

78   *Jack Pearce and the Chaddleworth Memorial (Photo by kind permission of Times Newspapers Ltd.)*

in a small cottage only a few yards from the
memorial bearing his and his brothers' names.

At the outbreak of war Jack and his brothers
were serving in India with the Royal Berkshire
Regiment and returned to France to take part
together in their first battle. In that battle Jack was
injured and his two brothers killed. After
recovering from his wounds he returned to the
front and was later wounded again. He had been
transferred to the Hampshire Regiment and so
presumably lost contact with anyone from his
home area, and had also during the war met his
future wife, whom he married in 1918, and spent

his periods of leave with her on the Isle of Wight
instead of in Chaddleworth.

And so, when they returned to the village as
husband and wife some time after the end of the
war it was discovered that Jack had been assumed
killed with his brothers in that first battle and that
his name had been inscribed with theirs on the
memorial of the village where he has lived since.

The memorial cross at Dilton Marsh in
Wiltshire lists over forty men of the parish who
fell in the First World War. This seems a very large
number for the size of the village.

A photograph taken at the scene during the

79   *Dilton Marsh, Wiltshire*

80 *The Crossmichael Memorial, Galloway, with the four McLelland names*

unveiling ceremony, shows a large crowd gathered, and, in the background, buildings which mostly still exist today.

One change in the scene is unfortunate in its effect on the visibility of the monument. Trees now surround the cross and, although they are in themselves attractive, they overhang it to the extent that it can now be seen clearly only from directly in front and no longer from the position of the 1920's photographer.

The war memorial in the village of Crossmichael near Loch Ken in Galloway, was unveiled on 11th December, 1921, by a Mr. McLelland who lost four sons in the war.

The granite Celtic cross from a design recommended by A. E. Hornel, the famous artist of the Glasgow School who had local connections, is on an elevated site on the outskirts of the village.

The main inscription reads —
CROSSMICHAEL HEROES' WAR MEMORIAL. 1914-1918. LEST WE FORGET.
and the names of the 41 men of the village who died have been added.

The names of the nine officers and N.C.O.'s are on the front of the memorial, and those of the other ranks on the sides.

On one side are found the names of the four McLelland sons, David, John and Robert, of the Gordon Highlanders, and Johnstone of the Highland Light Infantry.

In the churchyard of Henbury Parish Church near Bristol is another war memorial cross, and amongst the names carved on the base are those of three brothers, Edgar Parsons, Ernest Parsons and Milton Parsons, who all died in the war. In fact, another brother died after the war as a result of his wounds, and so, eventually, all four sons of the family were lost as a result of the conflict.

The memorial cross at Haughton, near Stafford, has eleven names of the fallen inscribed on its base. Three of these are of one family, John George (Jack) Redfern, Alfred Redfern, and William Gordon Redfern.

Jack was killed at Ypres on 9th July 1915 when aged 21, Alfred died near Lens on 26th

81 *Jack Redfern, killed at Ypres*

82 *Alfred Redfern, killed at Lens*

November 1916, and William was killed near Arras on 25th April, 1917, leaving a wife and two young daughters, one of whom he never saw. Two other brothers survived the war. Inscribed on the base above the names are the words,

WENT THE DAY WELL
WE DIED AND NEVER KNEW
BUT WELL OR ILL ENGLAND
WE DIED FOR YOU

The cross, which was erected in 1920, was re-sited in 1977, within the village, for traffic reasons.

At the start of the First World War a large number of soldiers were billeted, many sleeping in barns, near the tiny village of Eggington in Bedfordshire, and a wooden framed message was hung in the vestry of the village church reading:

"The European War 1914–15.

The Officers, N.C.O.'s and Men of the Troops 21st Division, stationed at Eggington during this winter, desire to place on record their appreciation of the generosity of the Vicar in placing this church at their disposal for Divine Services on Sundays, and for the many other kindnesses received during the whole period of their stay."

The Eggington Vicar's personal involvement with the war can be seen even more clearly by an examination of the stone cross near the churchyard gate which, together with a framed Roll of Honour hung inside the church, was erected as the village war memorial after the war. Four local lads had given their lives and one of those four named on the cross is that of A. J. E. Sunderland, the son of the vicar.

Mrs. Hilda Jones (née Coombes), now approaching 80, can remember her father's name being engraved on the war memorial at Shipton-under-Wychwood in Oxfordshire. She sat by the stone-mason's side, proud of the engraved name but barely realising the full implication of what was happening.

Her father was killed by a sniper at Gaza on 22nd December, 1917, a month after his brother died at Arras.

83   *The Shipton-under-Wychwood Memorial. Hilda Jones is on the right*

Hilda and another little girl whose father had died in the war, unveiled the memorial when the ceremony was held in 1921.

The memorial in Marston Moreteyne, in Bedfordshire, has engraved on it the names of 43 men who fell in the First War.

A photograph, taken at the memorial's unveiling by the Duke of Bedford, shows quite a different scene from that of today, when houses occupy the fields which at that time bordered the memorial. The impressive motor cars parked in the country lane alongside the memorial site at the time of the unveiling ceremony, can perhaps be assumed to belong to the official party.

The minutes of the War Memorial Committee for Scaleby in Cumberland show that its first meeting was on 26th April, 1919. Early discussions concerned the type of memorial to be chosen, and the suggestions were a wayside cross, a lychgate, a children's playground and a tablet in the church. The cross was chosen and a further meeting in July considered the various quotations received, which seemed to vary from £60 to £450.

84   *The Marston Moreteyne Memorial, Bedfordshire*

It was agreed to inscribe names but not ranks on the stone. Subsequent meetings in August and February 1920 dealt with the question of the names to be included on the memorial and the correct initials of the men in question; the latest financial statement, £133 having been collected by February; and the inclusion in the scheme of a commemorative tablet in the church and a gift for each of the men who served.

After a June meeting to settle details of the ceremony, the unveiling took place on 12thJuly, 1920. A Celtic Cross of grey Scottish granite was unveiled in front of the Parish Hall by Sir Robert Allison who had, in fact, given the hall to the village. On the memorial were the names of the 30 men from the village who had served, two of whom had died.

Silver match-boxes were then given to each of the men or to the families of the fallen, each box bearing the man's name and the date "1914–18." Afterwards refreshments were served in the Parish Hall.

The minutes of a meeting on 21st August, 1920, show the financial position to have been satisfactory; £100 had been paid for the Memorial to Beattie & Co. of Carlisle, £28 17s. 3d. to Walker & Hall for the match boxes, 18/- for the printing, and there was a balance of £11 16s. 6d. Quotations ranging from 6 guineas to 10 guineas for a tablet for the church were then considered.

The war memorial cross set in a pretty roadside garden in Marazion, the Cornish village near St. Michael's Mount, is unusual for its interesting ironwork surround. In particular, the wrought iron gate includes the words and musical notes of *Abide With Me, Fast Falls The Eventide*.

86   *Acomb Memorial after renovation*

Acomb, on the outskirts of York, was at the time of the Great War a village of some 3,000 people, and shortly after the end of the war a memorial cross was erected on the village green, just as similar memorials were being erected at that time in villages throughout the country.

Over the years the stone of the cross on Acomb Green weathered badly, until recently it was almost impossible to read the names of the 77 dead of the First World War or of those of the Second.

Fortunately, the grandson of one of the men commemorated launched a campaign to restore the memorial, and York City Council agreed to a sum of £5,000 being allocated to the cleaning of the cross and the re-carving of the inscriptions. This combination of individual enterprise and civic responsibility has led to a complete restoration of the monument.

The village of East Brent in Somerset has an unusually ornate war memorial for a village of its size. Standing by the roadside is a stone cross at the base of which are four stone figures of a soldier, an airman, a sailor and a merchant sailor.

Inscribed on the base are the words —
TO THE GLORY OF GOD AND IN PROUD AND GRATEFUL MEMORY OF THE FOLLOWING SOLDIERS FROM OR CONNECTED WITH THIS PARISH WHO GAVE THEIR LIVES FOR THEIR COUNTRY IN THE GREAT WAR 1914-1918.
YE THAT LIVE ON MID ENGLISH PASTURES GREEN REMEMBER US AND THINK WHAT MIGHT HAVE BEEN.

The names of seventeen such men appear on the memorial, to which have subsequently been added one from the Second World War and one from the Korean.

The joint population of Great and Little Kimble, villages which adjoin the Chequers estate in Buckinghamshire, was at the outbreak

85   *Acomb Memorial, York, before renovation*

87   *The East Brent Memorial, Somerset*

was necessary, and plans were adopted, sadly but unavoidably, to rebuild the cross to a shorter design.

The attractive war memorial cross beside the chestnut trees and pond on the village green at Writtle, in Essex, was restored in recent years by local people, amongst them the 2nd Writtle Girl Guides, who took upon themselves the task of cleaning the monument. At the same time others repainted the lettering and tidied the flower beds and general area. Such work has been carried out on many similar memorials but few sites justify it more than that in the centre of this pretty village (see Plate C12, p.61).

The war memorial in the village of Wheatley near Oxford was originally erected at Magdalen College, where it stood in front of the west door of the chapel, having been unveiled by the Prince of Wales in 1921.

It was not the college's only war memorial and had been removed during the Second World War and was still in a stone-mason's yard in the mid-1970's.

Wheatley had stong connections with Magdalen as the college had considerable land holdings there, and also because early parts of the college were built from stone quarried in the Wheatley area.

Therefore, when it was found that Wheatley's war memorial was in a dangerous condition, and that restoration work was going to be very costly, the village successfully negotiated the permanent loan of the unused Magdalen cross.

It was duly erected not far from the original memorial in the burial ground off the High Street. The old monument was subsequently removed and the burial ground made into a Garden of Remembrance. The transferred memorial was altered very little, the stem of the cross being shortened slightly and one tier of steps removed, and, later, slate name plaques were added and a service of dedication held.

The former Magdalen cross stands very well now in its attractive, well-tended garden with, on the base, the inscription,

THIS MEMORIAL, ONCE AT MAGDALEN COLLEGE, COMMEMORATES THE INHABITANTS OF WHEATLEY WHO GAVE THEIR LIVES IN TWO WORLD WARS. 1974.

The war memorial in the churchyard of St. Mary and St. Andrew in Grantchester, near Cambridge, is a limestone foliated cross on a base with inscribed panels.

There are the names of 17 men who died in the Great War, a large number for such a small village, and also the words "Men With Splendid Hearts" from the poem *The Old Vicarage, Grantchester* by Rupert Brooke, whose name is one of those seventeen inscribed.

At the village of Knowlton, near Canterbury, there is a memorial which to us nowadays, particularly with our knowledge with hindsight of the appalling losses of the Great War, might seem peculiarly tasteless.

The memorial is, in fact, the prize in a competition conducted by a weekly newspaper of the time and the inscription reads —

of war in 1914, only 530, yet 84 men went to fight for their country and the names of 8 of them are inscribed on the local memorial. This was unveiled in October 1920 by the Lord Lieutenant of Buckinghamshire, the Marquis of Lincolnshire, and is in the form of a medieval cross of Doulting stone with panels of Westmoreland slate. It was designed by a local resident, C. M. O. Scott.

At the time of the unveiling ceremony one of the speakers, Lord Lee, said that the memorial stood "on historic ground within a few yards of Great Kimble Church where John Hampden had raised his banner of freedom nearly 300 years ago." In fact, a statue of Hampden stands a few miles away at Aylesbury in the Market Square and only yards from the Aylesbury war memorial.

In his speech, Lord Lincolnshire referred to the fact that owing to the 'Liberality' of Lord and Lady Lee, "the old red house would for ever become the residence of the first minister of the Crown."

In recent years the memorial was cleaned and repaired, having become rather untidy, but ironically, shortly afterwards, in April 1987, gales snapped the cross pillar from its base and it was broken in four pieces. And so once again repair

and the words
ONE CROWDED HOUR OF GLORIOUS LIFE IS WORTH AN AGE WITHOUT A NAME.

The cross is by the roadside on the outskirts of the village, and the grass verge, and the hedge surrounding the memorial, are overgrown and unkempt.

Photographs taken at the dedication of crosses in several villages within a few miles of each other in Suffolk, have survived in good condition.

90   *The Darsham Memorial, Suffolk*

The village war memorial cross in the churchyard of All Saint's Church, Darsham in Suffolk, was dedicated on Sunday, 27th June, 1920.

Two photographs taken that day show a general view of the crowd gathered round the memorial during the service, and a group of some of the bereaved behind the cross after the wreaths had been placed.

In the first photograph the family in the

88   *The Knowlton Memorial, Canterbury*

THIS CROSS WAS ERECTED IN HONOUR OF THOSE TWELVE MEN OF KNOWLTON, OUT OF A TOTAL POPULATION OF THIRTY-NINE, WHO ENLISTED PRIOR TO MARCH 1915 AND BY THEIR PATRIOTIC ACTION WON *THE WEEKLY DISPATCH* BRAVEST VILLAGE COMPETITION.

Also inscribed are the sculptor's name
G. FRAMPTON, R.A. 1915

89   *The Darsham Memorial, Suffolk*

91   *The Stradbroke Memorial, Suffolk*

foreground to the right, gathered round a pram, is that of Mr. E. Green, who is still an inhabitant of the village.

During the service the Rev. Dr. Tennant appealed to the people of the village to care for the memorial, and its present condition shows that his appeal was heeded. It, and the churchyard entrance, look unchanged over the seventy years since the photographs were taken.

The ceremony of unveiling and dedication of the war memorial in the Suffolk village of Stradbroke was held on 30th July, 1922.

A photograph taken at the time shows a village street and churchyard not markedly different from the scene today. One difference in the appearance of the cross itself, is that the railings separating it from the churchyard are no longer there, but have been replaced by a very high evergreen hedge.

A photograph of the cross in the churchyard at Martlesham in Suffolk shows a typical scene as those present gather behind the memorial, after

the wreaths have been laid at its base.

The photograph is dated 19th December, 1919 and so the occasion would appear to be the service of dedication.

Finally, a very clear photograph has survived of the dedication service of the war memorial for the tiny village of Burgh, near Woodbridge in Suffolk.

Dedicated in September 1919, the granite cross was thought to be the first memorial erected in the diocese, and its position, on a corner adjoining the churchyard of St. Botolph's Church, is still a prominent one today.

The photograph shows Canon Page (Rector of Clopton), the Rev. G. M. Shallard (Rector of Burgh and father of the lady who owns the photograph), Mr. Mark Barlow of Hasketon, and Captain Sutton Smith D.S.O., R.N., as well as the families of the five men commemorated.

Three miles north of Ipswich is the tiny village of Akenham. There is no village street, just scattered cottages and farms, and a church

92   *The Martlesham Memorial, Suffolk*

93   *The Burgh Memorial, Suffolk*

standing in fields away from the main roads.

Six or seven men left this village to go to war in 1914–18, and three died. The war memorial in the churchyard gives their names. They were all brothers — Amos Purkiss, George James Purkiss, and Philip Edgar Purkiss.

Ironically, in such a secluded spot, the memorial cross has been knocked from its base, presumably by vandals, and now lies on its side. Fortunately, a tablet inside the church bears their names and the dates of the war.

The memorial at Kippax, near Leeds, is another which has suffered in recent years from vandalism. The monument is in the form of a staged plinth surmounted by the stone figure of an angel.

Two out of the three name-plates are missing and one of the arms of the statue has been broken off completely, while the other has been damaged.

94   *The damaged cross in Akenham, Suffolk*

95   *The Kippax Memorial, near Leeds*

96　　*The West Hallam Memorial, Derbyshire*

Monuments featuring sculptured figures are, perhaps, after crosses, the next most common form of village memorial.

The village of West Hallam in Derbyshire has a well-preserved memorial surmounted by an unusual sculptured group of a machine gun crew with one man in a firing position and another erect. The tribute is to all the village men who served in the war but the nine who died are listed separately on the front of the base (see Plate C11, p.61).

A photograph supplied by the daughter of the then rector of the parish shows, on the extreme left, the Bishop of Derby and her father on the occasion in 1920 or 1921 of the dedication of the memorial. With them on the platform is the rest of the official party whilst on the higher ground to the rear stand the choir and local councillors. At the edge of the crowd, in front of the platform, can be seen at least two members of the local wolf-cub pack.

The memorial in the Worcestershire village of Catshill was unveiled on Sunday, 2nd October, 1927, by Major General Cayley, who had served for nearly 30 years with the Worcestershire Regiment. The dedication was by the Rev. S. R. James, the Archdeacon of Dudley.

The land had been donated but the memorial, which cost £250, was paid for by the local people. The money was raised by whist drives, concerts, bazaars, jumble sales, and a charity football match. £240 had been raised by the unveiling date and a collection among the crowd on that occasion raised a further £23.

A photograph taken in 1927 of a group in fancy dress publicizing a fund-raising event, shows the secretary of the committee, Charles Trevis, on a donkey, and the owner of the local cinema, Harry Bowers, in a clown's costume. Charles Travis had served as an officer with the South Staffordshire Regiment throughout the war despite being seriously wounded, and had spent two years after the war with the War Graves Commission.

97　　*Fund-Raising at Catshill*

98   *The Catshill Memorial, Worcestershire*

99   *The Kirkfieldbank Memorial, Lanark*

required to stay at home because of the need to provide material for the war effort, over one hundred from the village went to war and of that number sixteen were killed. Their names appear on the village war memorial on a site next to their former village school (see Plate C10, p.61).

Harry Bowers made a silent film of the fund-raising events which the villagers were to see later.

Similar enthusiasm is perhaps required again today. The memorial, the stone figure of a soldier with reversed rifle on a plinth bearing the names of 69 men who fell, is on a prominent corner site but the hedges and surrounds are very unkempt, to the point where it is difficult to see the lower part of the monument.

There are twenty-six names on the granite pedestal of the roadside war memorial in the village of Kirkfieldbank near Lanark.

The name heading the list is that of Sergeant J. B. ("Jock") Day who was apparently a magnificent figure of a man, the tallest for miles around. The eldest son of a woodcutter, he had emigrated to Canada just before the outbreak of the war but had still fought and died as so many, comparatively, from the village had done.

The memorial with its figure of a soldier with reversed arms, is surrounded by attractive railings and is well maintained.

Wanlockhead is in north Dumfriesshire and, said to be the highest village in Scotland, has a history of lead mining. Although some men were

100   *The Penpont Memorial, Dumfriesshire*

101
*St Margaret's
Hope
Memorial,
Orkneys*

The memorial is a marble figure of a soldier with rifle reversed and facing the high hills beyond the village. The figure stands on a marble base on the foot of which are inscribed the words
DULCE ET DECORUM EST PRO PATRIA MORI,
(It is sweet and glorious to die for one's country).

At the unveiling ceremony on the 19th September, 1920, about one thousand people were present.

The war memorial in Penpont in Dumfriesshire is to the memory of 41 men of the village. On a rough stone base is the 1920 bronze statue by Kellock–Brown of a soldier with rifle reversed and head bowed in mourning.

A photograph of the war memorial unveiling ceremony at the village of St. Margaret's Hope, on South Ronaldsay in the Orkneys, shows both the official party and the monument itself very clearly.

102
*The Oban
Memorial,
Argyll*

60

C8   *St. Anne's, Turton*

C9   *The Royal East Kent Regiment Memorial*
        (Photograph — R. Bettison)

C10   *Above: The Wanlockhead Memorial*
C11   *Above right: The West Hallam Memorial*
C12   *Right: The Writtle Memorial*

C13 *The Sonning Memorial*

C14 *The Flackwell Heath Memorial*

C15 *The Grange-over-Sands Memorial*

The gentleman in uniform was the headmaster of the local school, the girl to the right of the memorial carried out the unveiling having lost three brothers in the war, and the clergymen were from the various churches of South Ronaldsay.

The details of the memorial can be clearly seen. On a base of rough stones stands the figure of a Highland soldier in stone, the work of Alexander Carrick R.S.A., R.B.S., 1882-1966, who worked on many memorials of the Great War, both in stone and in bronze.

Similar figures in stone to the St. Margaret's Hope one were made by Carrick for Killin in Perthshire and for Loch Awe where the statue stands on the water's edge. Another of his works in stone is the unusual and striking group of two Highlanders carrying a wounded comrade between them, which, on a base of rough boulders on the seafront, forms Oban's impressive tribute.

Amongst the artist's bronze figures are two great-coated soldiers at Walkerburn in the Scottish Borders, and at Blairgowrie in Perthshire, each soldier with arms reversed, coat collar up and head bowed. Another fine bronze statue is at Dornoch where a Highland soldier, with one hand raised to shield his eyes from the light, looks out towards Dornoch Firth.

104   *The Dornoch Memorial, Sutherland*

103   *The Blairgowrie Memorial, Perthshire*

105   *The Frazerburgh Memorial, Aberdeen*

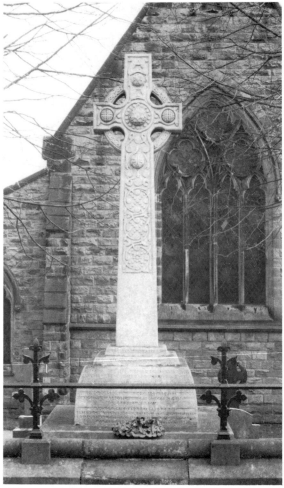

106   *The Berwick Memorial, Northumberland*

107   *The Quarndon Memorial, Derbyshire*

On the high pedestal of the memorial are the words,

ON FAME'S ETERNAL CAMPING GROUND THEIR SILENT TEARS ARE SPREAD.
AND GLORY GUARDS WITH SOLEMN ROUND THE BIVOUAC OF THE DEAD.

Quite different works in bronze by Carrick, are the group symbolic of peace on the Frazerburgh monument, and the Angel of Peace in Berwick.

It is, however, for his work on the Scottish National War Memorial at Edinburgh Castle that Alexander Carrick is perhaps best known. On the front elevation of the building the two figures of "Justice" and "Courage" are his, while inside, the bronze panels to the Royal Engineers and the Royal Artillery (in which he himself served) are also his works.

108
*Ashbourne,
Derbyshire*

109   *The Sennen Memorial, Cornwall*

Many other artists or firms were each responsible for several memorials. The cross in the churchyard at Quarndon, Derbyshire, is one of several war memorials made by Messrs. W. E. Lomas of King Street, Derby. Mr. J. Lemmings, now in his 80's, was apprenticed as a carver and letter cutter to the firm in 1920 and whilst getting used to the tools was given the task of roughing out and then carving the faces of a number of crosses and memorials.

Several, like that at Quarndon, were of a design based on the Cross on the Isle of Iona. Made in local Hopton Wood stone (Limestone), there are examples in Derby and Heanor as well as in Quarndon.

A quite different type of war memorial made by the firm is that of the Memorial Gateway of red Hollington stone in the Park at Ashbourne.

The memorial at Sennen is the nearest to Land's End and stands in the churchyard of the Parish Church inside which is a framed roll of honour listing all the men who served in the war. A granite cross, it is the work of William Arnold Snell of the Newlyn firm of W. H. Snell & Son which was responsible for many Cornish war memorials.

Amongst them are those at Mousehole, Newlyn, Pendeen, Ruan Minor, Sancreed, Morvah, Madron, St. Just, Hayle, St. Erth, St. Mary's Church, Penzance, Gulval where his notes suggest a price of £50 for a granite memorial with 100 letters inscribed, and for further letters a charge of 8/- per dozen, and at Penzance where, because of its exposed position, the memorial had to be constructed like a lighthouse, the stones dove-tailed to each other with two bronze pins in each stone.

Mr. Snell also went further afield, the memorials at Bideford and West Bromwich, for example, being made by him.

The Cornishman of the 10th December, 1964, reports him still working at the age of 74, recutting the slate plaques for the Penzance memorial and complaining that he could not get on quickly enough with the 800 or so letters because of the poor light at that time of year.

Photographs taken on the day of the unveiling of the war memorial in the Warwickshire village of Hampton-in-Arden, show both the ceremony itself and the parade of ex-servicemen just before the ceremony began.

The memorial, on a prominent roadside site at a junction in the village, is a Portland stone cross made by J. White & Sons, stonemasons of South Yardley, Birmingham. This firm was

110   *The Mousehole Memorial, Cornwall*

111
*The Newlyn
Memorial,
Cornwall*

founded in 1866 and the grandson of the founder retired in 1968. This grandson, Mr. Leslie White, at the age of almost 90, remembers some two dozen memorials of the Great War made by the family firm. The majority of these are in Warwickshire although there are others in Forres, Scotland; Halifax, Yorkshire; Staffordshire and Shropshire.

The memorials range from crosses of Cornish granite or Portland stone like that at Hampton-in-Arden, to Yorkshire stone cenotaphs like that at Halifax, and from Cornish granite obelisks like the cyclists' memorial at Meriden to Portland stone wall tablets like that in the pretty hilltop church at Preston Bagot in Warwickshire.

112
*The
Hampton-in-
Arden
Memorial,
Warwickshire*

113
*The
Hampton-in-
Arden
Memorial,
Warwickshire*

THIS TABLET IS ERECTED IN DEEP THANKFULNESS TO ALMIGHTY GOD FOR MERCIFULLY DELIVERING US FROM OUR ENEMIES AND PRESERVING OUR LAND FROM INVASION AND IN MEMORY OF THE MEN FROM THIS PARISH WHO FELL IN THE GREAT WAR

1914 - 1918

2ND LIEUT ARTHUR DENZIL ONSLOW M.C. R.WAR.R.
PRIVATE DICK NEALE   R.WAR.R.
PRIVATE CLEMENT JAMES JONES   SOM.L.I.

IN CHRIST SHALL ALL BE MADE ALIVE

114
The Preston Bagot Memorial, Warwickshire

Churches are frequently the sites of such village memorials. Just over the border between Shropshire and Wales, and a few miles from Welshpool, is the tiny village of Criggion.

In the beautiful little church of St. Michael's, at the foot of Breidden Hill, is a brass tablet commemorating the four men of the parish who died in the war, three of them being brothers, Albert, Thomas and George Phillips, and the fourth Trooper Frank Williams of the 20th Hussars.

115   *The Cadmore End Memorial, Buckinghamshire*

At the unveiling ceremony on 3rd April, 1921, about 60 ex-Servicemen marched in procession from the school to the church behind the Glyn Ceiriog Band playing *Onward, Christian Soldiers.*

The local newspaper reported that after the service "the band marched the Comrades to the schoolroom to partake of a sumptuous tea."

The same report referred to the fact that "the vicar, in reading out the names of the fallen heroes, was deeply affected as he spoke of them and their loss to their parents and the parish."

A most attractive and unusual village memorial is to be found in the church at Cadmore End in Buckinghamshire. A font-cover statuette made from silver and bronze given by villagers in memory of their dead, it was the work of a local sculptress, Kathleen Shaw. Models for the Virgin Mother and baby represented, were a Miss Kitty Keen and baby Margery Saunders, apparently the only baby of suitable age, at that time, in the village. The child's uncle, Walter James Druce, is one of the nine men commemorated, their names appearing on the octagonal base cover, along with their regiments, date and place of their death, and their age at the time. Further Second World War names have been added.

In the village church at Sonning in Berkshire the names of the dead of the war are set in marble tiles in a line along one wall of the church. Each tile has the name of one man together with his regiment and regimental badge, the date and place of his death and his age. One, for example, reads

WILLIAM BRIND ROYAL BERKS. KILLED IN ACTION AT ARRAS 24th APRIL 1917. AGED 25.

The regimental badge of the Berkshires is in the top left hand corner of the tile. There are twenty such tiles and others have been added in similar style for the dead of the Second World War (see Plate C13, p.62).

On Remembrance Sunday a glass is placed on a shelf under each memorial and as each name is read out a young member of the congregation (recently the local Brownie pack has performed

116
The Yoxall Memorial, Staffordshire

the duty) steps forward and places a poppy in the appropriate glass. A basket of poppies is placed under a central tile which reads

IN PROUD AND GRATEFUL MEMORY OF THE MEN OF THIS PARISH WHO FELL IN THE GREAT WAR 1914-1918.

The Parish Church in the village of Yoxall, near Lichfield, has a war memorial window, and an alabaster plaque listing the names of the thirty officers and men who died in the war. The window shows a wounded soldier looking up at a crucified figure of Christ, while the plaque is a very ornate one with the carved figure of an officer on one side and that of an infantryman on the other. Between these figures the thirty names are listed in order of rank. Amongst the privates are J. H. and C. J. Lester, whose sister still helps in replacing the flowers at the foot of the memorial window.

In addition, the village has a monument erected by public subscription to the 130 men of the community who served in the war. This is in the form of an obelisk which stands in the grounds of the Parish Hall.

Sometimes, the village memorial is itself a hall.

Above the entrance door to what is commonly known as "The Institute" in the village of Esholt near Bradford, is a stone inscribed

IN MEMORIAM 1914-1918

and with the names of four men from the small community who died in the war, for the building is, in fact, the War Memorial Hall.

Inside the building is a list of all the 53 villagers who served in the war.

The hall was apparently built largely with stone given by Bradford Corporation, and by the use of voluntary labour. The hall is still very much used by the villagers, and also by the cast of the television programme *Emmerdale Farm*, much of which is filmed at Esholt.

The war memorial in the beautiful little Cornish village of Crantock is a Memorial Hall in the centre of the village. The hall is a small, attractive, well-kept building with an entrance

117 *The Memorial Hall, Crantock, Cornwall*

118
The Upper Ballinderry Memorial, Co. Antrim

porch above which stands a cross.

The names of the five fallen of the First War are inscribed above the entrance door. There are also inscribed round the sides of the door seven names from the Second War, more deaths, unusually, than in the First.

The laying of the foundation stone of the War Memorial Hall at Upper Ballinderry, Co. Antrim, was on 4th July, 1924. A photograph of the occasion shows Mrs. M. A. Walkington presenting a trowel to the gentleman entrusted with the ceremony, Mr. Alfred Sefton.

The hall, inside which is a brass tablet with the names of the men commemorated, has subsequently been used for many activities such as dances, bazaars, meetings and badminton and, more unusually, for housing evacuees for a time after the Second World War bombing of Belfast.

The village of Flackwell Heath near High Wycombe had already completed one war memorial scheme, a Parish Memorial Hall, by the time the second was dedicated in May 1921. This is an obelisk of Portland stone about 9ft. high, the head of which, a ball upheld by four crosses, represents the world supported by the cross. The monument was designed by Thomas Thurlow of High Wycombe and the work was carried out at a cost of approximately £100 by H. T. Dickens of High Wycombe.

On the memorial there are the names of some 50 men from the village who lost their lives in the war, including four brothers, Albert, Frederick, Owen and William Rogers. After the Lord Lieutenant of Buckinghamshire, the Marquis of Lincolnshire, had unveiled the obelisk, the Marchioness expressed a desire to meet Mr. Albert Rogers, the father of the four brothers. A report in the *Bucks Free Press* of May 13th, 1921 goes on, "It was a pathetic incident as the Marchioness who had lost her only son (Viscount Wendover) in the war expressed, with tear dimmed eyes, her heartfelt sympathy with the aged father and the members of the family. It was an incident that will not be readily forgotten by the assembly."

Today the memorial is surrounded by a beautifully-kept attractive garden and is a credit to the whole village (see Plate C14, p.62).

Other villages found the idea of an obelisk, or similar monument, to be attractive. Footdee is in the St. Clements' Ward of Aberdeen District Council and is a small sea-side village built in 1808 and consisting of about eighty houses, all of which are apparently now listed.

Its war memorial, which was unveiled as early as 16th August, 1919, is a granite obelisk with bronze plaques, one with the figure of a soldier and one with that of a sailor, while on the base are thirty-five names from the Great War.

The work was the gift of a Mr. Caie who was born in the village and owned the Pittodrie Granite Works.

119   *The Footdee Memorial, Aberdeen*

69

120
*The Canisbay
Memorial,
Caithness*

The nearest war memorial to John O'Groats is at the small village of Canisbay, Caithness, a few miles along the shores of the Pentland Firth and near the Queen Mother's home, the Castle of Mey.

There are over forty names, mostly of Seaforth Highlanders, on the polished granite monument which was unveiled on 14th September, 1921, by Lord Horne. The memorial is of an unusual design and surmounted by an urn, and it has been erected on a comparatively elevated and isolated site on a moorland road some way out of the village. Despite its exposed position, the column is wearing well because of the material of which it is made, but nevertheless some decoration seen on the photographs of the unveiling is no longer so clearly visible.

The small village of Durisdeer, in Dumfriesshire, is a community which, because of disagreement about the best choice of site for the war memorial, finally compromised by having two.

Next to the Parish Church in the heart of the village is a rough-hewn granite column with the figure of a soldier in relief. The column and plinth are on a rough white marble base and the bronze name plaque lists thirty-three names of the men from the parish who died in the war.

Fully two miles away, on a roadside site by the A702, is a second memorial, this time in the form of a granite obelisk on a decorated plinth.

121   *The Durisdeer Memorial, Dumfriesshire*

122   *The Hartwell Memorial, Northamptonshire*

This monument is in a well-tended area with newly painted railings and trimmed privet but, strangely enough, the names on this memorial are not the same as those near the church. There are only twenty-eight names listed here, with the names of Henry Lockhart, Francis McJannet, John McJannet, George Rogerson and Alex Rogerson all missing.

The village of Hartwell in Northamptonshire, is another where there was a division of opinion concerning the choice of site for a war memorial, leading to the most inappropriate controversy and even bitterness.

One group of parishioners were in favour of a cross in the local churchyard "Surrounded as it would be by the last resting places of the forefathers of the fallen."

Others, however, were in favour of a wooden monument in a more prominent position in the centre of the village, and since neither group would give way or compromise, eventually each erected its own independent tribute.

The idea of trunks of timber for a memorial came from the fact that the village was famous for its timber from the adjoining Salcey Forest, but the wooden structure erected in 1920 did not wear well, and by the end of the Second World War the timber was described as decaying and dirty, the surrounding wooden railings as dilapidated, and the area as choked with weeds.

Eventually the memorial was apparently replaced by a virtually identical one, and both that and the churchyard stone cross are now in reasonable condition, although the wooden one, with its wooden surround, will obviously always present a maintenance problem.

On the wooden memorial a brass plate with the names of the three dead of the Second World War has been added to the similar plate with the names of the eleven dead of the First, and this memorial is still used annually for the official Remembrance Service.

The village of Ampthill, in Bedfordshire, is a third which has two war memorials as a result of a disagreement between various factions in the village after the war.

A large area called the Alameda was offered to the village council by the Duke of Bedford as a gift, and it was agreed to erect a monument on part of it, and also to establish in the village an ex-servicemen's club or hostel.

However, many wished to have a memorial in the form of a cross erected in the churchyard, and the clergy wrote a joint letter to the local newspaper.

"The proposal to erect a War Memorial in the Alameda has been associated with a subsidiary scheme to establish a hostel for ex-soldiers . . . to take the form of a registered club, at which intoxicating liquors will be sold on weekdays and Sundays, without the restrictions attaching to the ordinary public house . . . We consider the result of its establishment would be most injurious to the best interest of Ampthill."

Eventually a monument in the Alameda was unveiled on 17th May, 1921, by Princess Beatrice, a daughter of Queen Victoria. She later formally declared open the United Services Club in a large house offered for that purpose in Church Street. The memorial dedication was performed by the Chaplain General of the Forces, Bishop Taylor-Smith.

The architect who designed the memorial was a Professor A. E. Richardson but several features of the entrance gates which he suggested are no longer to be seen.

Two stone vases purchased at his suggestion for £20, and stone ball finials which were also described, are sadly no longer part of the gates.

A week after the unveiling of the Alameda memorial, Lord Ampthill unveiled a cross in the churchyard. The architect for this memorial also was Professor Richardson, who appears to have been almost alone amongst those involved in the discussions on choice of idea, in not violently objecting to at least one of the two conflicting schemes.

The village of Hutton Magna in North Yorkshire has an unusual war memorial in the form of a lychgate by Thompson of Kilburn, better known for his woodwork and carvings in

124   *Hutton Magna Memorial, North Yorkshire*

125   *The Sandridge Memorial, Hertfordshire*

Ampleforth College, and for his furniture with its typical mouse "signature."

The lychgate is at the entrance to the parish church, and inside the gate is a panel carved with the names of the 12 men from the village who fell in the war. Three of the men, Jack, Bertie and Gilbert Hind were brothers, and the uncles of the present churchwarden, Marian Lewis.

Another name is that of Lieutenant R. W. M. Close, whose father, the Rev. W. A. M. Close, was vicar of Hutton Magna for over thirty years.

Due to the Rev. Close, the Roll of Honour accompanying the village memorial is unusually well-documented, and in the vestry of the church is a framed photograph of each man commemorated, together with biographical details.

Another memorial in the form of a lychgate is that at Sandridge, in Hertfordshire, at the entrance to St. Leonard's Church.

The names of the dead, and of the men who served and returned, are on tablets on the supporting wall of the lychgate and under the roof of the timber construction.

Carved in the wood on the face of the memorial are the words

THROUGH THE GRAVE AND GATE OF DEATH WE PASS TO OUR JOYFUL RESURRECTION.

The war memorial in the Sussex village of Bodiam, looks at first sight to be a lychgate. Situated by the roadside, the structure surmounted by a cross, encloses not a gate, however, but the village pump.

A brass plate on the pump commemorates

126   *The Bodiam Memorial, Sussex*

the names of the fallen and tells that the memorial was dedicated by parishioners and friends in October 1922.

At the edge of the village of Crossford, near Lanark, is the Crossford, Hazelbank and District war memorial with its twenty names of those from the area who fell in the First World War. The memorial is a cross built into a curved wall and surrounded by railings. An unusual feature is that it incorporates a drinking fountain.

Minutes of the war memorial committee show the early discussions on the type and position of the proposed tribute and the early fund raising efforts. Most of the income was from individual contributions but a football match between Crossford and Netherburn raised the princely sum of £4-7/-.

The records include the contractor's final bill which, with various additional items, amounted to £342-17-6d. The builder was Robert Speedie of Crossford.

The unveiling was on 21st May, 1922, and the account from J. Bell of Carluke, the printer employed, shows items of £5-9/- for 500 programmes, 9/- for 24 invitations and envelopes and 11/- for advertising in the local press.

A bugler and three pipers attended the ceremony and as well as the Last Post, the lament *The Flowers o' The Forest* was played.

In 1976 the Parks Department of Lanark District Council took over the upkeep of the memorial, and the Church took on the duty of supplying the poppy wreath each year.

They are to be congratulated, both on the condition of the memorial, which appears to have been recently renovated, and on the particularly beautiful wreath placed at the last Armistice anniversary.

Another roadside drinking fountain on the edge of the village of Gwernymynydd in North Wales, is the war memorial to the eight men of the village killed in the Great War. The structure of stone blocks, surmounted by a small Celtic Cross, and enclosing a tablet with the names of the fallen and the fountain itself, was unveiled on Saturday, 5th August, 1922.

Although crosses and sculptured figures make up the majority of village memorials, a great deal of imagination went into planning appropriate tributes, and a wide range of ideas resulted.

The village of Ruyton-XI-Towns in Shropshire has a most unusual memorial. When, in earlier times, a road was carved out of the red sandstone known as The Brownhill, a 30ft. cliff was left on one side. The war memorial is in the form of a cave cut into this solid rock, with the dates 1914-1919 carved above the entrance.

The cave is about 8ft. deep and at the back is carved a large cross, while on either side is a stone seat. Above the left-hand seat is a tablet with the coat of arms of the County and the borough, and the names of the seventeen men who fell in the war. The tablet also commemorates 130 other men who served.

A London architect, Stanley Griffiths, designed the memorial which was made by local stone-masons and unveiled in October 1920 by General Kenyon, with buglers of the King's

128   *The Ruyton-XI-Towns Memorial, Shropshire*

73

Shropshire Light Infantry sounding the Last Post.

On the outskirts of the small Yorkshire village of East Keswick, near Wetherby, is a memorial cross with a plaque inscribed,

THIS MONUMENT IS ERECTED AND THE LIME TREES PLANTED TO THE LASTING MEMORY AND UNFADING GLORY OF THE MEN OF EAST KESWICK WHO GAVE THEIR LIVES IN THE GREAT WAR 1914-1918.

There are 17 names on the cross and in the early 1920's a line of trees was planted, stretching from the memorial along one side of the main road leading out of the village, and each tree carried a name plate with the name of one of the fallen. Today half a dozen name plates are missing, and some of the trees are now showing the first signs of age, but although nature may eventually remove the line of trees, nevertheless the stone cross will remain, and to the relatives of the men who died, the combination of trees and cross must have seemed a fitting and original way to commemorate them.

In the meantime, it would not be a difficult or expensive task to replace the missing name plates and repair several others which require attention. The memorial is, in fact, maintained "by a legacy from the late Mrs. G. M. Dickenson of this village 1973", so cost may not be a consideration.

The pretty village of Canwick is on high ground overlooking the City of Lincoln a mile away. In its small churchyard is a memorial which is very unusual in its design, and which is certainly not instantly recognisable as a 20th century war memorial. It was in fact designed by S. Parvin of Turner, Lord & Co., London, and made by M. Tuttell & Son, Lincoln. The central feature is the shrine proper, which is 15th century Italian work in wrought iron upon which is placed a figure in ivory of the crucified Christ. Above this is a gilded figure in wood representing the risen Christ.

The shrine is enclosed in an ornate Portland stone canopy with carved pinnacles and gables. Three sides of the memorial are open between

130   *The Canwick Memorial, Lincolnshire*

the canopy supports, while the fourth is filled by the slab on which are carved the names of the eight men from the village who died.

131   *The Withern Memorial, Lincolnshire*

Two of these were brothers who were both Lieutenants in the Irish Guards. Francis Leslie Melville Pym was reported missing near Ypres on 2nd July, 1916, aged 21, and his brother Claude John Pym, died near Albert on 26th March, 1917, aged 24.

At the unveiling soon after the war in June 1919, the prayers of dedication were pronounced by their cousin the Reverend T. W. Pym, D.S.O., who had been Senior Chaplain to the 3rd Army.

At a public meeting at Greystoke in Cumberland on the 24th May, 1919 it was decided that the War Memorial should take the following form:

"1. That a Brass Tablet be set up in the Parish Church recording the names of all men of this Parish who have given their lives in Active Service during the War.

2. That a second Brass Tablet be set up in Penruddock Church recording the names of those of the above who came from that side of the Parish.

3. That a bridge suitable for wheeled traffic be built over the Wath at Greystoke Church to take the place of the existing foot bridge — thus making a safer and more appropriate approach to the ancient church; and that a copper plate should be fixed on the parapet of the bridge, with a suitable inscription.

And that contributions towards the cost of the memorials be invited from every householder and inhabitant of the Parish."

The scheme was carried out at a total cost of some £400 and the unveiling ceremony attended by the Bishop of Carlisle was on 8th May, 1921.

The plate in St. Andrew's Church, Greystoke, carries the names of 16 men who gave their lives in the war, and the copper plate on the bridge describes the background to its construction.

The war memorial at Withern in Lincolnshire is a Calvary at the side of the main road. The site is a prominent one and the memorial, surrounded by railings, is well-kept and tidy. In addition to the Calvary, a brass plate was erected in St. Margaret's Church, but some years ago this was closed and the tablet removed to the local chapel.

The Reverend G. H. Holmes, who was born in 1907, remembers the Calvary being dedicated and the hymn *O Valiant Hearts* being sung. His late father had a small harmonium which he remembers being carried from their house for the dedication service. After working in several parishes he has returned to retire in the cottage where he lived as a boy.

The memorial to the eleven men of the village of Naseby, in Northamptonshire, who fell in the war, was erected in March 1921. Made of

132
The Naseby Memorial, Northamptonshire

mellow Northamptonshire stone, it features a recumbent lion, and it has been said that "the choice of a rather tired lion, though somewhat unusual, was not inappropriate."

The monument occupies a prominent position at a road junction, in the village near which one of the decisive battles of the Civil War had been fought.

The records of the Royal British Legion branch at Lustleigh in Devon include the indenture between Major-General William James Fawcett of "St. Andrews", Lustleigh, and the trustees of the Lustleigh British Legion, conveying free of charge the land upon which the local war memorial was afterwards built.

The conveyance was dated 17th March, 1924 and on the 28th November, 1924, a letter from the Newton Abbott Rural District Council approved the proposed plans, copies of which are also still preserved.

The two most striking features of the memorial based on those plans are the massive rough-hewn central boulder in which a cross is carved, and the attractive use made of a hillside site.

134   *The Sledmere Memorial, Yorkshire*

133   *The Lustleigh Memorial, Devon*

In the village of Sledmere, in the Yorkshire Wolds, there are two unusual memorials to the Great War, only a few yards apart.

The first, opposite the entrance to the church, is a Queen Eleanor Cross, 55ft. high and of Portland stone, which was built in 1899 by Sir Tatton Sykes. The upper stages of the cross have at each face the figure of a Queen, but the lower faces of stone have been used to commemorate various individuals, chiefly men of the 5th Yorkshire Regiment or employees on the Sledmere estates, who gave their lives. The likeness and figure of each has been reproduced on a memorial panel (see Plate C16, p.95).

One panel is inscribed,
REMEMBER EDWARD BAGSHAWE CHAPLAIN OF THE 5th YORKSHIRE REGIMENT KILLED IN FLANDERS ON JULY 22nd 1916.

Another,
THE NAMES INSCRIBED ON THIS CROSS ARE THOSE OF OFFICERS AND MEN OF THE 5th YORKSHIRE REGIMENT WHO GAVE THEIR LIVES FOR THEIR KING THEIR COUNTRY AND THE LIBERTIES OF MANKIND IN THE YEARS OF THE GREAT WAR.

Yet another reads,
LT. COL. JAMES MORTIMER COMMANDED 5th YORKSHIRE REGIMENT 1915 — SEPTEMBER 15th 1916, ON THE MORNING OF WHICH DAY HE WAS KILLED IN ACTION ON THE SOMME. ON HIS LEFT HAND STANDS CAPT. FRANK WOODCOCK, 5th YORKSHIRE REGIMENT, WHO FELL A FEW HOURS AFTER ON THE SAME DAY IN THE SAME PLACE. BEHIND STANDS LANCE CORPORAL HARRY WOODCOCK, PRINCESS PATRICIA'S CANADIAN LIGHT INFANTRY, WHO FELL MAY 8th 1915 AT THE 2nd BATTLE OF YPRES. BOTH BROTHERS-IN-LAW OF THE ABOVE.
THESE EFFIGIES WERE RAISED BY DORA MORTIMER, WIDOW OF JAMES MORTIMER, AND ELIZABETH JANE WOODCOCK, HER MOTHER, AND BROTHER AND SISTERS.

At the feet of two of the figures are white roses of York, and under the third is a maple leaf.

Finally, amongst other panels is one commemorating Lt. Col. Sir Mark Sykes, the M.P. for Central Hull, who served as commander of the 5th Yorkshires until being moved to Staff duties. He died suddenly in February 1919 when in attendance on the Peace Conference in Paris.

135　　*Waggoners' Memorial, Sledmere, Yorkshire*

136　　*A detail from the Waggoners' Memorial*

The second memorial in the village was designed by Sir Mark Sykes himself

AS A REMEMBRANCE OF THE GALLANT SERVICES RENDERED IN THE GREAT WAR 1914–1919 BY THE WAGGONERS' RESERVE, A CORPS OF 1,000 DRIVERS RAISED BY HIM.

These skilled men from the Yorkshire Wolds were not only raised but also trained by him, in fields close to the site of the memorial. They went to France early in the war and casualties were heavy. The monument is to both the fallen and the survivors, and was erected by Lady Sykes and unveiled in September 1920 by Lieut. General Sir Ivor Maxse, C. in C. Northern Command.

Executed by Carlo Magnoni of London, and Mr. A. Barr, the estate mason, the memorial is 20ft. high, of Portland stone, and carries a series of carvings depicting the activities of the Waggoners from peace time to enlistment, from the farewells to their families to their landing in France, and from early scenes of action and of German atrocities in France to the Waggoners driving the enemy back across the Marne.

Regular reunions of the Waggoners have been held over the years but this year it was planned to hold a final official reunion, on August 7th 1988, when the last of the group, believed now to be five in number, were to be guests of honour at Sledmere House.

Chapter VI

Small Towns

For the purpose of this limited survey a "small town" is taken to be one which, at the outbreak of the Great War, had a population of less than 40,000. It would not have the atmosphere or integrated nature of a village, nevertheless there would still be a greater awareness of everyday affairs and a greater involvement in the whole community than would be possible in the large towns and cities.

Areas which were virtually no more than part of a large industrial city are excluded from this category.

In these smaller towns decisions about war memorial schemes tended to be made quickly, and memorials were usually erected in the first few years after the end of the war, while in some cities discussions alone went on for years, and schemes were still incomplete a decade after the Armistice.

Nowadays, although vandalism is widespread and no area can claim to be immune, nevertheless it is in the large towns and cities that the situation is most serious, while in the small towns and, of course, in villages, when damage to memorials does occur and when there are instances of graffiti, then it is more normal for repair or cleaning to take place promptly.

As in the case of villages, crosses and sculptured figures make up the majority of memorials in small towns, crosses again being most common.

The war memorial at Woodbridge in Suffolk, in a well-kept garden setting with the parish church in the background, was unveiled in November 1920.

The cross of Weldon Stone, brought from Northamptonshire, has inscribed on its octagonal base the names of 133 men of the town who fell in the war.

The unveiling was performed by the Earl of Stradbroke who had just been appointed Governor-General of Victoria, and so was shortly to leave for Australia, and the dedication prayer was recited by Archdeacon F. J. Clarke.

At the four corners of the cross, sentries, members of the Officer Training Corps of Woodbridge School, stood with reversed arms and bowed heads, and the Excelsior Band, which still exists today, accompanied the hymns and played solemn music.

A booklet about the ceremony and the memorial was printed and proceeds from the sale were given to a fund for assisting children of the men who had died.

The Newquay memorial is in a dominating position on the Headland overlooking both the sea and the town. A cross mounted on a cairn of granite, it is on the site of the "Old Look-Out House", an admiralty building of some antiquity which stood previously in that position. It was unveiled by the Prince of Wales, Duke of Cornwall, on Tuesday 24th May, 1921. The

137
The Woodbridge, Memorial, Suffolk (Photo by kind permission of Woodbridge Museum)

78

138   *The Prince of Wales at Newquay*

139   *The Newquay Memorial*

photographs shown here were taken on that day by a woman whose brother had died in the war.

The first Warwick memorial to the Great War was a wooden plaque fastened to the railings of St. Mary's Church on Sunday, 18th March, 1917. This was a gift from Lady Nelson and unveiled by the Mayoress, Mrs. Airth-Richardson. The tablet bore the names of about 12 officers and 200 men who had been killed in 1914, 1915 and 1916. By this time there were about 1,300 Warwick men, out of a total population of some 12,000, serving in the armed forces.

140   *The Warwick Memorial*

In 1920, after a meeting to discuss the type of memorial required and the most appropriate site, a design submitted by Mr. C. E. Bateman, F.R.I.B.A., of Birmingham was accepted. It was of a 36ft. high cross pierced in 14th century Gothic style, and the estimated cost was in the region of £2,000 for which amount an appeal was launched.

A list of 312 names of the fallen appeared in the local press in February 1921 along with a request that relatives of those not listed should apply for inclusion of their names.

The cross was subsequently unveiled on Sunday, 10th July, 1921, by Lord Percy, but it was not until November 1923 that the Mayor, Dr. Tibbits, closed the appeal for finance by personally paying off the deficit still remaining of £21-12-11d.

The attractive monument in Portland stone, with the names on four bronze panels, is situated in Church Street, at the corner of the churchyard of St. Mary's. Having been recently cleaned the memorial looks exactly today as it did in early postcards.

In St. Mary's Church itself there are several Great War memorials, including one to the Royal Warwickshire Regiment, and one to the Yeomanry.

The cross in Loftus, near Whitby, to the 87 men who died in the war, was designed by B. J. Wormleighton and erected on land given by Lord Zetland.

The memorial booklet, issued at the time of the unveiling ceremony on Armistice Day 1922, includes the Roll of Honour printed under the words of Rupert Brooke,
"These laid the world away,
Poured out the red sweet wine of youth,
Gave up the years to be of work and joy,
and that unhoped serene that men call age."

141
*The Loftus
Memorial,
near Whitby,
North
Yorkshire*

The cross stands on an elevated roadside site in the centre of the town, and is approached by a curved staircase on either side.

The surroundings are more attractive now than in old photographs, with more extensive and mature gardens flanking the memorial, and with a row of houses, formerly immediately behind the monument, no longer stretching that far. To the rear of the memorial now can be seen the gardens of a nearby church.

Mr. & Mrs. Andrew Williams were married on 26th June, 1869, in Cheltenham, and celebrated their diamond wedding whilst living at Woodbine Cottage, Charlton Kings, Gloucestershire, when he was 86 years old and she was 79 and both were described as "hale and hearty." He had been a gardener at Ashley Manor for 25 years, and at 86 still tended his own large garden himself.

They had brought up a family of 11 children but lost four sons, a son-in-law, and a grandson in the war.

The names of three sons, Frederick, Frank and Louis, and of the son-in-law James Jeffery, are on the well-tended and prominent memorial cross at a fork in the road at St. Mary's, Charlton Kings' Parish Church.

The other son Charles lived elsewhere in the country as did their grandson. Yet another son,

William, the father of the grandson who died, was himself badly injured and in a wheelchair for many years before his death in the early 1940's.

As a tribute to their great sacrifice, Mrs. Williams was asked to represent the people of Charlton Kings at the unveiling of the memorial in the early 1920's.

To judge from old photographs, the setting of the war memorial cross at Grange-Over-Sands on Morecambe Bay, has changed little over the years. The stone cross, on its stepped base, stands in attractive gardens surrounded on three sides by the waters of a pleasure lake (see Plate C15, p.62).

The memorial cross on its seafront site at Sandown, Isle of Wight, was unveiled on Monday, 25th July, 1921, by Princess Beatrice with the words,

"In the name of all who are gathered here and of those who belong to this town, we unveil this Memorial and solemnly dedicate it to the Glory of God, and in grateful and imperishable memory of those whose names it bears."

The Silent Prayer which followed, was introduced,

"Let us now be quiet and ponder in our hearts the fact that we owe our freedom to the heroism of those who gave their lives, and in silence let us thank God for all that they were and did."

142
*Sandown
Memorial, Isle
of Wight*

An unusual tribute is that of the Memorial Grove at Kingston Vale, on the edge of Wimbledon Common and close to Richmond Park. The Grove is in the centre of 42 acres of playing fields and land which are themselves part of the memorial.

At the dedication service in July 1925, conducted by the Bishop of Southwark, Dr. Garbett, credit was given to the efforts of Mr. Richardson Evans who had been largely responsible for the scheme and for its fruition.

In the centre of the circular Grove itself, a cross of Cornish granite was built and inscribed,

THE LAND AROUND, 42 ACRES, IS DEDICATED TO THE PUBLIC USE IN MEMORY OF ALL THOSE WHO, HAVING BEEN RESIDENT OR BELONGING TO FAMILIES RESIDENT IN THE ADJOINING DISTRICTS, GAVE THEIR LIVES FOR THEIR COUNTRY IN THE GREAT WAR 1914-1918.

Amongst the names commemorated by the cross are those of two V.C.'s, J. S. G. Dimmer, and A. L. Harrison, although the names on the plinth have suffered badly from weathering.

Another inscription, words of Richardson Evans himself, reads,

NATURE PROVIDES THE BEST MONUMENT, THE PERFECTING OF THE WORK MUST BE LEFT TO THE GENTLE HAND OF TIME.

Ironically, severe gales in the autumn of 1987 uprooted several of the trees in the Grove and brought down branches from many others.

The Roehampton war memorial cross, on Roehampton Common just above the village, was partially destroyed by enemy action in 1941, later restored, and re-dedicated in 1952, on Armistice Sunday.

144   *The Roehampton Memorial*

145   *Knaresborough, the original Cross*

The original unveiling and dedication were by the Princess Alice, Countess of Athlone, and the Vicar of Roehampton, Canon Browne, on Thursday, 27th July, 1922.

The architect, Laurence Turner, based his design on an early 15th century cross in Bishops Lydeard, Somerset, and on the shaft of the Portland stone cross he incorporated four niches in which were carved, not separately but out of the same block of stone, the figures of the two soldier saints, St. George and St. Michael, and the figures of a Soldier and a Sailor.

Unfortunately, not all of these figures have survived completely undamaged, although generally the memorial shows little evidence of its narrow escape from complete destruction.

An inscription on one side of the memorial reads,

THE NAMES ARE RECORDED IN THE VILLAGE CHURCHES.

Another memorial which has suffered damage is that at Knaresborough, in Yorkshire.

An old photograph shows an elegant and well-proportioned structure, with a long, slender, decorated shaft terminating in an elaborately designed cross.

Today the same memorial, in the attractive Castle grounds, has a quite different appearance. The base and the plinth, with the inscribed name plates, seem to be unchanged, but some 30 years ago a severe gale destroyed the top section of the monument and it has been replaced by a much shorter and simpler shaft and by a very ordinary cross.

The Prime Minister, the Right Honourable David Lloyd George, unveiled the Thame war memorial on Saturday, 30th July, 1921, and during his speech referred to the fact that out of a population of less than 3,000, just over 600 men from Thame were in the services during the war years, and of these 600, 87 were killed or died of wounds, and over 200 were wounded.

Photographs show that the monument, near the centre of the town, has changed little over the years, except that the railings which existed at the time of the unveiling are no longer there, although a metal gate remains, flanked by a low wall.

The memorial, a Portland stone cross and base, was designed by J. T. Robinson and cost between £800 and £900, not all of which had been

147   *The Thame Memorial, Oxfordshire*

collected by the time of the unveiling, although no deficit was anticipated in the long term.

An old photograph of the stone Celtic cross that is the war memorial of the small North Yorkshire town of Leyburn, shows that the buildings around it have changed little over the years. The number of vehicles in the market-place, however, is very different, with the area at peak times, nowadays, almost completely occupied by parked cars.

The memorial cross in the churchyard of Benton near Newcastle was unveiled by an ex-serviceman, Thomas Nicholson, who had lost both his legs in the war.

The inscription on the base includes a reference to those "who died from wounds and are buried in this plot", and engraved stones, set into the well-tended area around the memorial, with its attractive flower beds and lawn, mark the graves of those who had presumably returned to this country before dying of their wounds.

The Hereford County and City War Memorial was unveiled in St. Peter's Square, Hereford, on 7th October, 1922. "The Order of Proceedings" shows that Lt. Colonel Gilbert Drage, D.S.O., unveiled the monument which was then dedicated by the Bishop of Hereford.

The memorial, over 30ft. in height, takes the form of an Eleanor Cross, with figures of a soldier, a sailor, an airman and a nurse in four niches of the central section. On panels below, in relief, are eight badges, those of the Herefordshire Regiment, the Royal Army Service Corps, the Royal Air Force, the Royal Artillery, the King's Shropshire Light Infantry, the Royal Engineers, the Royal Navy, and the Royal Army Medical Corps. Shields displaying the arms of the City of Hereford and the See of Hereford appear on the central section, above which is an open lantern surmounted by a dome and cross.

On one side of the plinth are inscribed the words

149
*The Benton
Memorial
unveiling,
Northumber-
land*

83

150 *Hereford Memorial*

TO THE MEN OF HEREFORDSHIRE WHO FELL IN THE GREAT WAR 1914-19

and on the opposite face

THEIR MEMORY HALLOWED IN THE LAND THEY LOVED

adapted from John S. Arkwright's *Supreme Sacrifice*.

The memorial, made principally of stone from the Darley Dale quarries, with sculptured figures of Portland stone, was designed by Mr. L. W. Barnard of Cheltenham.

St. Albans' elegant war memorial cross, set in a pretty and well kept Garden of Remembrance, is situated at St. Peter's Green, with the 15th century St. Peter's Church in the background. The tribute to over 600 men killed in the First World War was unveiled by the Earl of Cavan and dedicated by the Bishop of St. Albans, on Sunday, 22nd May, 1921 (see Plate C17, p.95).

Two V.C.'s are amongst the dead commemorated. Lieutenant A. V. Smith of the East Lancs. Regiment died on 22nd December, 1915 in the trenches at Gallipoli when he threw himself on a bomb which was about to explode, and Private A. Warner of the 1st Bedfordshire Regiment died of wounds and gas poisoning near Ypres on 1st May, 1916 after holding a trench single-handed against repeated attacks.

The records show what appears proportionately to be an unusually large number of brothers who died during the war. Of course, no national statistics exist for accurate comparisons and it is not possible to rely purely on surnames on memorials to make assumptions, even when those surnames are very unusual ones, but detailed records exist in the archives of many towns, St. Albans included.

Amongst many such instances at St. Albans are two twins, Cecil Arthur Bailey and Guy Frederick Bailey M.C. The former, a 2nd Lieutenant in the 4th West Yorks., died whilst attempting to save his orderly on 6th May, 1915, aged 18, and his brother, a captain in the York and Lancaster Regiment, was killed near Lens on 7th July, 1917.

Three Catlin brothers died, A. F. Catlin on 25th January, 1917, E. Catlin three weeks later on 15th February, 1917, and J. T. Catlin on 21st October, 1918, just before the end of the war.

W. A. Corley and P. M. Corley died on the same day, 25th September, 1915, one with the Rifle Brigade, and one with the 2nd Border Regiment.

Three Hart brothers were killed, W. P. on 25th May, 1915, H. C. on 3rd September, 1916, and E. on 6th July, 1918.

L. V. Kent and H. Kent died within four days of each other, on 31st July, 1917, and 4th August, 1917.

E. B. Sharp was "murdered by the enemy at the sinking of the S.S. *Belgium Prince*" on 3rd July, 1917, and in the following month H. Sharp was killed on 16th August, 1917.

A final example is that of two brothers killed on the same day and in the same battalion. A. E. and J. W. Smith of the 124th Canadian Pioneer Battalion, who died on 6th November, 1917.

In addition to the memorial at St. Peter's Green, St. Albans, about a dozen street memorials were also put up in the town and

151 *St. Albans Street Memorial*

84

152
Altrincham and the Chapel Street Memorial

153   *Huntingdon Memorial*

many remain to this day, although some wood and glass ones have disappeared over the years and one, in Lower Dagnall Street, was obliterated by the householder on whose property it was placed, leaving only a rough concrete slab to show where it had been.

Amongst others, memorial tablets in Bardwell Road, Sopwell Lane and Albert Street, are all still well preserved, with the names on them clearly visible to commemorate the men from those streets who died in the war.

The Altrincham war memorial, a Celtic Cross with a low surrounding wall set in an attractive well-kept Garden of Remembrance, has to one side of it what at first sight appears to be a notice board, but is in fact a framed Roll of Honour to the men of one street, Chapel Street. Before Chapel Street was demolished because of re-development the Roll of Honour was on the wall of the Wesleyan Chapel at the corner of the Street.

On the occasion of the unveiling of the Roll of Honour on the 5th April, 1919, by the Earl of Stamford, a letter was sent from Buckingham Palace to the people of Altrincham. It is still on display in the Town Hall and part of it reads,

"I am commanded to convey the thanks of His Majesty to the inhabitants of Altrincham for their loyal assurances . . . and the King congratulates them and especially those living in Chapel Street that out of 60 houses 161 men served in the war, 30 of whom made the supreme sacrifice."

It now seems beyond belief, that, on average, nearly three men from each house went to war, and that, on average, one household in every two had someone to mourn by the end of 1918.

Sculptured figures on memorials of the Great War are, naturally enough, often those of soldiers in the uniform of the time.

Huntingdon's war memorial, a statue known as "The Thinking Soldier", was unveiled

85

154   *The Elland Memorial, near Huddersfield*

by the Lord Lieutenant of the County, the Earl of Sandwich, on Armistice Sunday 1923 in the presence of some 3,000 people, and was immediately acclaimed as a beautiful and inspiring tribute. A gift from the Huntingdonshire Federation of Women's Institutes, it was sculpted by Kathleen Scott, the widow of Scott of the Antarctic. The artist must have received undue attention from the press as she apparently addressed the *Huntingdonshire Post* photographer as "You awful man."

In the press report of the ceremony particular mention was made of the wreaths and other floral tributes which were placed at the foot of the memorial, with simple bunches of flowers next to official wreaths such as the Lord Lieutenant's. Unusually, an attempt was made to provide a comprehensive list of these tributes amongst which were —

"In remembrance, from the officers, warrant officers, N.C.O.'s and men, 5th Huntingdonshire Regiment."

"Huntingdon Branch British Legion. In undying memory of our unconquered comrades who gave their lives for our safety.

Au Revoir. Till Gabriel sounds the Rally."

"In loving memory of those Wesleyan lads who nobly fought for their country but did not return."

"In remembrance, 2nd Hunts. Grammar School Scouts and Cubs."

"From the Huntingdon Town Football Club to our fallen comrades who 'played the game'."

"In devoted memory of my Billie — Mrs. W. P. Markwich."

"To our dear daddy from his little children. Bertie and Connie Strangward."

The war memorial at Elland, near Huddersfield, is on a commanding hill-top site at the entrance to a public park.

The memorial was designed by F. W. Doyle Jones in 1922 and has a granite plinth supporting the realistic bronze figure of a soldier in full uniform, standing at ease with his rifle in front of him and with the collar of his greatcoat turned up. The whole impression is of a phlegmatic and most determined character.

The names of about 180 men who fell are inscribed on the plinth which is beginning to show signs of deterioration. Gaps are beginning to open between the various blocks of granite and maintenance work should not be long delayed.

The war memorial in Enniskillen, County Fermanagh, was the scene on Remembrance Sunday, 8th November 1987, of an I.R.A. bombing which resulted in the death of 11 people of the town. The explosion, at 10.45 that morning, destroyed St. Michael's Reading Room, the local community centre, and brought part of it crashing down on the crowd waiting for the Remembrance Ceremony which was soon to have taken place a few yards away.

Debris covered the area and flying fragments pockmarked the stonework of the memorial, inscribed with the names of the war dead. Bandsmen left their pipes and drums to search with bare hands for bodies and survivors amongst the ruins.

Two weeks later, on Sunday 22nd November, with the debris cleared away and the site of the explosion boarded up, the Remembrance Ceremony finally took place, in front of a huge crowd. The ceremony was attended by the Prime Minister and a photograph taken that day shows Mrs. Thatcher laying a wreath at the base of the memorial beneath its bronze figure of a Royal Inniskilling Fusilier, whose regimental motto was NEC ASPERA TERRENT (Neither do difficulties deter).

The main feature of an attractive monument in a corner of the park at Clayton-le-Moors, in Lancashire, is a bronze group of a soldier with helmet and rifle, and a female figure with one hand on his shoulder and appearing, with her other hand, to be pointing out to him the way ahead.

The original bronze plaques on the plinth have been replaced by panels of slate, and on one is the inscription,
PASS NOT IN SORROW BUT IN LOWLY PRIDE AND STRIVE TO LIVE AS NOBLY AS THEY DIED.

The war memorial at Thornton Cleveleys,

155   *Mrs. Thatcher laying a wreath at Enniskillen (Photo by kind permission of Times Newspapers Ltd.)*

near Blackpool, is in a prominent roadside position and surrounded by the flower beds and lawns of a well-tended and attractive garden. The bronze figure of a soldier, bare-headed and with rifle reversed, is on a tall plinth on which are inscribed the names of the men from the area who died in the war.

An unusual feature is that the names of the dead of the Second War are listed on massive stone books set between the flower beds surrounding the original monument (see Plate C19, p.95).

The memorial at Farsley, near Leeds, was erected in June 1921 on a corner site outside what was then the Farsley Council Offices.

The names of the fallen are inscribed on the plinth, on top of which is the stone figure of a soldier in greatcoat and cap, and with rifle reversed and head lowered.

The names from the Second War have been added and on the wall of the building in the background is a plaque commemorating the men of the South African war.

The statue is surrounded by well-maintained railings and attractive flower beds.

The Inverary war memorial stands on the edge of Loch Fyne with the steep hill of Duniquoich in the background and Inverary Castle close by.

The bronze figure of a Highland soldier on a base of rough-hewn boulders, the 1922 memorial is the work of sculptor Kellock-Brown.

As well as the bronze name plaques a further plaque carries the words,
IN MEMORY OF THOSE YOUNG LOVED LAMENTED HERE WHO DIED IN THEIR COUNTRY'S CAUSE 1914-1918.

The memorial in Annan, near Dumfries, was unveiled on 4th December, 1921, by Lieutenant General Sir Francis Davies who at the time was G.O.C. Scottish Command. The bronze figure of a Borderer in full service kit sculpted by H. Price of London, stands on a pedestal of grey Creetown

156
The Clayton-Le-Moors Memorial, Lancashire

157   *The Farsley Memorial, Leeds*

158   *The Inverary Memorial, Argyll*

159   *The Annan Memorial (Photograph — R. Cawood)*

granite erected by Orlando Rae of Annan. The height of the memorial is 17ft. and the cost was £1,700.

On the front of the pedestal are inscribed the words, GLORIOUS THEIR FATE, on the sides, SPLENDID THEIR DOOM and GIVE THEM PRAISE NOT PITY, and on the rear HONOUR THEM AND WEEP NOT.

The Dumfries memorial was unveiled on Sunday, 9th July, 1922, also by Lieutenant General Sir Francis Davies, G.O.C. Scottish Command and, after the dedication by Reverend J. Montgomery Campbell, Provost Macaulay accepted custody of the memorial on behalf of the town council. The Lament at the ceremony was played by the K.O.S.B. pipe band, and the figure on the memorial is in fact that of a soldier of the K.O.S.B. The figure is 7ft. high and the whole monument with its pillared base, is of Creetown granite, and one of many made at the Bon-Accord Granite Works, Aberdeen, of Messrs. Stewart & Co.

On the base are the words —
MAY THEY SLEEP IN HONOUR UNBETRAYED AND WE IN FAITH AND HONOUR KEEP THAT PEACE FOR WHICH THEY DIED.

The memorial at Maxwelltown near Dumfries, like that in Dumfries itself, came from the Bon-Accord Granite Works of Stewart & Co. However, in the case of the Maxwelltown memorial, the figure of a soldier which stands on the granite pedestal is not itself of granite but of bronze, and is the 1921 work of sculptor Henry Price.

The figure is a particularly fine and moving piece of sculpture. The young soldier is in full uniform but without a rifle, and his arms are

160   *The Dumfries Memorial*

photographs shows a sequence of events which was repeated over and over again throughout the country at the time of the First World War.

The first photograph shows the Town Council and townspeople, on a railway platform, seeing off a group of young men in uniform and with their kit bags at their feet, early in the war.

The second shows the funeral procession of Private Charles Riddock of Portsoy. He died of wounds on 22nd May, 1918 aged 27. It appears from the photograph that a large proportion of the community turned out to pay their respects.

The final photograph is of the unveiling of the war memorial on 10th November, 1923, and of pipers playing the lament. The memorial statue, made of grey Creetown granite, is of a Gordon Highlander in full uniform with arms reversed and head bowed, and a large proportion of the names on the memorial base are of Gordon Highlanders.

The monument was made and erected by Messrs. Stewart and Co. of Aberdeen and unveiled by Colonel J. J. George of Macduff, Deputy Lieutenant of Banffshire, who was introduced by Provost John Rae.

Today the statue and its surround look exactly as they did in 1923. The whole area is immaculately kept and even the railings and nearby buildings are unchanged.

The Burslem, Stoke-on-Trent, war memorial incorporates a fine stone figure, of a soldier with rifle reversed and with his head bowed and bare, his helmet lying at his feet.

There are flower beds on either side of the memorial and also close by is the individual tribute to a Second World War soldier, Lance Sergeant J. D. Baskeyfield of the 2nd Battalion South Staffordshire Regiment who won the posthumous V.C. for his actions at Arnhem.

In one of the speeches during the unveiling ceremony of the war memorial at Blaydon near Newcastle, it was mentioned that out of the population of the town over 1,500 had joined the

raised towards heaven with the palms upwards, as if begging for an end to the slaughter.

Below him on the granite are inscribed the names of over 200 men of the burgh who fell in the war.

The monument, with a total height of 15ft, is on a prominent site at a road junction, and behind it is an attractive and well-tended garden of lawns and rose-beds. Anyone visiting the memorial must feel that everything about it is as the men commemorated would have wished it to be.

Portsoy is a small port on the Moray Firth, a few miles from Banff. A series of old

161
The
Maxwelltown
Memorial,
Dumfries

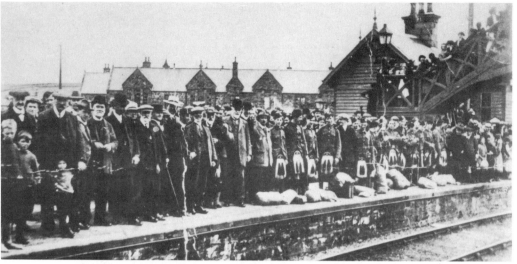

162
Portsoy, Banff

163
Portsoy, Banff

164
The Portsoy Memorial, Banff

colours, and over 300 fell. This is a very high proportion of dead, and in a Memorial Booklet there are, in fact, 308 names listed, including one nurse, May G. Brinton.

The unveiling, on 7th April, 1923, was performed by Miss J. Cowen, of Stella Hall, who had apparently contributed a great deal, both financially and otherwise, to the memorial scheme from its inception.

The memorial stands within the cemetery grounds at Blaydon, but in sight of the road which passes nearby. It is well looked after and impressive, its main feature being the great-coated figure of a soldier with rifle reversed and head bowed.

The unveiling of the Kendal War Memorial was on 1st July, 1921 and was carried out by Col. Weston M.P.

The figure of a soldier with rifle slung over his shoulder, the memorial stands in the Market Square which looks very similar today to its appearance in the photographs of the ceremony,

90

165   *The Burslem Memorial, Staffordshire*

166   *The Blaydon Memorial, Northumberland*

except that nowadays stalls and shoppers have replaced the official party on the platform, the organ on a cart, and the police and crowd of school children and townspeople watching the ceremony.

The bronze figure of a soldier in the main square of Truro is comparatively unusual in that the majority of such figures are fairly restrained and, in many cases, even standing with reversed arms in mourning. The Truro figure has one arm raised high in exultation, with the helmet held in the hand, and its spirit is perhaps close to that of "The Homecoming", the Cambridgeshire memorial.

The memorial in Newburn, near Newcastle, was unveiled on 15th July, 1922, by the Duke of Northumberland.

The monument, the stone figure of a soldier on a stone base into which are set bronze tablets, has unfortunately in recent years suffered, it would appear, from the attention of vandals. One hand from the statue is missing and the bayonet of the rifle is no longer there. Sadly, not all the name plaques remain, and it is to be hoped that adequate records exist elsewhere of the missing names.

Unless immediate attention and subsequent protection is given to the memorial, its future must be in grave doubt.

Three weeks after unveiling the memorial at Twickenham, Field Marshal Sir William Robertson unveiled that at nearby Richmond, on Wednesday, 23rd November, 1921. The Vicar of Richmond, the Rev. J. F. Kendall then offered the

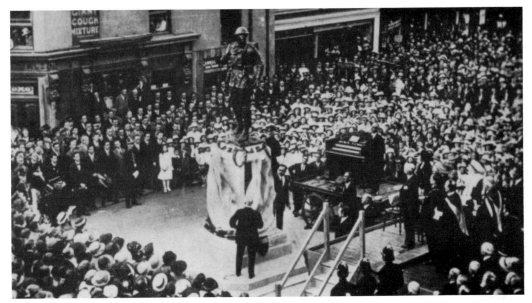

167
*The Kendal
Memorial,
Cumbria*

91

168   *The Truro Memorial, Cornwall*

169   *The Newburn Memorial, Northumberland*

prayers of dedication.

Designed by Mr. W. J. Pickering, the stone memorial, on a riverside site close to Richmond Bridge and the Town Hall, featured figures of a soldier and a sailor, and had flanking panels inscribed with the names of 708 Richmond men who had fallen.

After the service and the wreath-laying a procession of school children passed the new monument. The local newspaper reported the procession as "apparently endless" and in fact some 2,500 children took part.

The structure is at present hidden under wooden cladding for its own protection, as a major re-development of the area is taking place, and the spot is surrounded by building material and plant.

The memorial unveiled on 6th November, 1921, at Stalybridge in Cheshire, was designed appropriately enough, by a native of the town, an eminent London sculptor, F. V. Blundstone. His design, at one end of Victoria Bridge over the River Tame, consists of pedestals of stone at each side of the bridge, supporting groups of bronze statuary, one group representing the Army and one the Navy. The total height of each pedestal and bronze is 18ft. and from each pedestal a 5ft. high wing wall curves away to end in a smaller pedestal surmounted by a lion.

The wing walls carry the names of the 628 men who gave their lives, their names being arranged in regiments.

A public subscription raised £6,000 in a few weeks, and since this was almost 50% more than the cost of the memorial the surplus was devoted

170   *The Stalybridge Memorial, Cheshire*

92

171   *The Kirkcudbright Memorial*

to furthering the education and interests generally of the children of the fallen.

Sculptures of figures other than soldiers were also popular, with an artist such as Alexander Carrick, for example, producing works like those at Frazerburgh and Berwick, as well as soldier figures at Oban, Dornoch, Blairgowrie and many other places.

Maclellan's Castle is the site of the Kirkcudbright war memorial, and the massive bronze warrior of the memorial is similarly from an age other than that of the Great War.

On a base of rugged stones from the nearby seashore, the figure is seated with a sword in his right hand and with a child asleep against his knee. The sculptor, G. H. Pavlin of Edinburgh, was introduced to the town council by E. A. Hornel, the artist of the "Glasgow School," who had connections with Kirkcudbright.

The memorial was unveiled on 14th April, 1921, by Col. R. F. Dudgeon, the Lord Lieutenant of the county, and dedicated by the Reverend W. Barclay. Reports of the ceremony mention that amongst those present was a veteran of the Crimean War, the 87 year-old Robert Kissock Cameron.

The seafront war memorial in Troon, unveiled on Sunday, 30th November, 1924, by Brigadier General J. W. Walker, is a 10ft. 6ins. high bronze figure of Britannia on a granite pedestal, 13ft. high.

Britannia holds Victory in one hand and with the other holds out a palm in tribute to the town's dead who lie buried beyond the seas.

According to the Memorial Booklet, the aim of the sculptor, Walter Gilbert, was "to bring consolation to the bereaved, and an inspiration and an example to generations of the future."

The war memorial for Reigate and Redhill took the form of a Memorial Sports Ground at London Road, Redhill, and also a monument erected at Shaw's Corner, between the two present town centres.

Admiral of the Fleet Earl Beatty performed the unveiling ceremony on Sunday 5th August, 1923, before proceeding to London Road to declare the Sports Ground "open to the use of the public for ever, to commemorate the gallant deeds and sacrifices of those connected with the Borough who fell in the Great War."

The monument features the bronze figure of a man carrying a child, in one arm, whilst holding aloft a flaming torch with the other. He is striding forward, his face set and gaunt. The figure is on a granite plinth on which, in bronze, are the words, COURAGE, HONOUR and SELF-SACRIFICE.

172   *The Troon Memorial, Ayrshire*

173   *Reigate and Redhill Memorial*

In the Form of Service for the ceremony the monument is described as follows,

"The bronze group is intended to represent the triumphant struggle of mankind against difficulties that beset the path of life. Shielding and bearing onward the child, the figure holds aloft the torch of self-sacrifice, to light the way. The torch, used as a symbol, is a cross, enveloped in flames, which, though able to consume the body, cannot harm the spirit."

The bronze was by Richard R. Goulden, a former captain in the Royal Engineers, whose other work included a very similar figure in a beautiful Garden of Remembrance on the site of an old burial ground in Kingston-upon-Thames. Once again the figure holds a burning torch and strides forward, but this time the child is on foot at the man's side and looking up at his face.

Goulden also executed the figure of St. Christopher which is the war memorial of the Bank of England and, outside the Parish Church of St. Michael, Cornhill, in the City of London, the bronze winged and armoured saint with sword raised, which is the memorial to the 2,130 men from the offices in the parish, who volunteered to serve their country.

Also by Goulden, is the war memorial at Crompton, near Oldham, in an attractive and well-tended garden and consisting of a bronze group on a plinth of Scottish granite. The group represents man protecting the future generation in the form of little children, and clearing the perils in their path.

On the face of the granite is inscribed,

IN MEMORY OF THE MEN OF CROMPTON WHO FOUGHT AND GAVE THEIR LIVES TO FREE MANKIND FROM THE OPPRESSION AND BRUTAL TYRANNY OF WAR. 1914-1919.

94

C16   *The Sledmere Memorial*   C17   *The St. Albans Memorial*   C18   *The Hyde Memorial*

C19   *The Thornton Cleveleys Memorial*

C20   *Harrogate "1914 — The call to Arms"*   C21   *The Loughborough Memorial*

C22   *Top left:* **The Guildford Memorial**
C23   *Left:* **The Peterborough Memorial**
C24   *Above:* **The Woolwich Memorial**

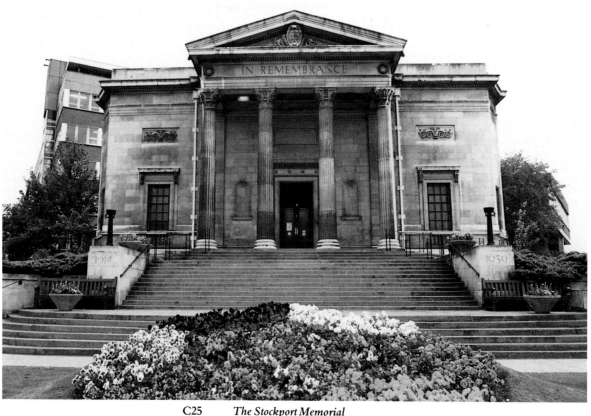

C25   *The Stockport Memorial*

174   *St Michael's Church, Cornhill*

175   *The Crompton Memorial, Lancashire*

On the sides are Rolls of Honour in sculptured bronze, each 5ft. in height and with relief panels depicting the heads of men from the various services. On these rolls are the names of 346 men including Alfred, Charles and Richard Hopley. Mrs. Hopley, who had eight sons serving in the war, laid one of the official wreaths when the memorial was unveiled by General Sir Ian S. M. Hamilton, and dedicated by the Vicar of Shaw, the Reverend A. R. Mackintosh.

Built into the structure was a sealed lead casket containing a variety of items, including various coins from a sovereign to a penny, three

cops of cotton spun in the district, a length of fustian cloth manufactured locally, wartime ration books, a programme of the local peace celebrations on 19th July, 1919, the first report of the Crompton Disabled Sailors and Soldiers Association, the 1922-23 yearbook of the Crompton Urban District Council, the Crompton Tradesmen's Almanac, a retail price list of provisions, a copy of a local newspaper, the names of the three oldest inhabitants in the area, and a summary of the war memorial scheme from its inception.

176
*The Dover
Memorial*

The Dover memorial, and the area surrounding it, have changed little since the photographs taken at the unveiling ceremony on 5th November, 1924.

The memorial is the bronze figure of a youth holding a cross aloft, the figure standing on a marble base to which are attached low walls carrying plaques with the names of the dead.

The building seen behind the statue in a contemporary postcard, looks identical today, except that there are now signs identifying it as the Dover Library.

The unveiling was carried out by Admiral Sir Roger Keyes, and the dedication by The Archbishop of Canterbury.

177   *The Folkestone Memorial*

Folkestone's tribute to its war dead stands on the Leas, 100ft. or so above sea level, and although the bronze female figure, which is the main feature, appears to be looking down, she is in fact looking towards the battlefields of Flanders. The sculptor, F. V. Blundstone, intended the figure to be a symbol of Motherhood and although in her right hand she holds a victory laurel, in her left she holds a cross attached to the shaft of which is a Union Jack at half mast as a symbol of sacrifice.

The memorial was unveiled in December 1922, by the Earl of Radnor and dedicated by Canon Tindall.

Stretching away down the hill to the harbour, is a road known as "The Road of Remembrance" because of the number of men who passed along it in the First World War on their way to France, from the camps in the area. The road is planted with "rosemary for remembrance" down one side, and a plaque at the top of the hill near Folkestone's war memorial explains the road's significance.

The Lewes memorial is in a prominent position in the town centre, on an island in the centre of the road and at the top of a hill. It is surmounted by a bronze winged figure holding aloft a laurel wreath and facing, across an unbroken view, the obelisk on Cliffe Hill which commemorates the seventeen Protestant martyrs of Queen Mary's reign, who were burned for their faith in front of what was then the Star Inn and subsequently became the Town Hall.

The names of the men of Lewes who also died for a cause are on bronze shields at the base of the monument and flanking bronze figures representing Peace and Justice.

The unveiling ceremony was by General Sir Henry C. Sclater on 6th September 1922 and the dedication was by the Bishop of Lewes. The Order of Service lists 237 men whose names are inscribed on the memorial.

178   *The Allerton Memorial, Yorkshire*

Over 100 men from Allerton, near Bradford, gave their lives in the war, and the memorial to them is situated just inside the entrance to Ladyhill Park. £2,000 was raised by public subscription for the monument which was designed by Harold Brownsword of London. A stone pedestal is surmounted by a group of three bronze figures, a boy symbolizing Posterity offering a laurel wreath in tribute to a soldier supported in the arms of a cowled figure of Death.

A lead-lined casket containing newspapers and a selection of contemporary documents was placed under the foundations of the memorial, which was unveiled on 29th July, 1922, by Sir James Hill, a freeman of Bradford who had risen from humble beginnings to become Lord Mayor. He had become M.P. for Bradford Central in 1916, and had been created a Baron in 1917. The dedication was offered by Rev. W. E. Spencer, and a poem specially written for the occasion was read by the poet Walter Robinson.

The Allerton memorial has in the recent past suffered from vandalism but, apart from a small amount of graffiti it is at present in a well-maintained condition.

The bronze group is a particularly interesting and imaginative work and its sculptor, Harold Brownsword, who was later principal of

179   *The Thornton Memorial, Yorkshire*

Regent Street Polytechnic in London, also designed two other local memorials, at Thornton and Eccleshill.

That at Thornton, near Bradford, is in the form of a bronze female figure on a high stone pedestal. The figure symbolising Peace, stands with the head bowed and with arms extended. In each hand she holds a laurel wreath.

The memorial, in Thornton Cemetery, but close to and easily seen from the main road, was unveiled on 30th September, 1922, by Albert Farrar, chairman of the responsible committee, and dedicated by the Rev. A. H. Tollit.

The third work by Brownsword is not, however, as well-preserved as the others. In a recreation ground in Eccleshill, near Bradford, it has been the target of vandalism over the years and attempts to have it re-sited in the grounds of Eccleshill Library have not been successful. Railings round the memorial are kept locked for obvious reasons, but the area is very untidy, name plaques are missing and it is difficult to read the inscriptions from outside the railings.

The monument, a bronze figure of Peace on a stone pedestal with flanking walls on which are the name plaques, was unveiled on 10th June, 1922, by the former Lord Mayor of Bradford, Lieutenant Colonel Alderman Anthony Gadie and dedicated by the Vicar of Bradford, Archdeacon W. Stanton Jones.

The memorial at Calverley, near Bradford, is near the entrance to Calverley Park and was unveiled on 27th May, 1922, by Ralph Grimshaw, president of the local ex-Servicemen's Association, and dedicated by the vicar, Canon C. H. K. Broughton.

A bronze female figure symbolising Patriotism, on a Portland stone pedestal, holds a laurel wreath in her right hand and, in her left, a small winged Victory. The designer was Lewis Frederick Roslyn, a London Sculptor, who had been commissioned into the Royal Flying Corps, and who worked on war memorials as far apart as Trinidad and Cape Town.

180   *The Calverley Memorial, Yorkshire*

Another work of his in the Bradford area was at Greengates, in a small garden by a main road junction. This was unveiled on 5th November, 1921, and is a high narrow shaft of stone on top of which is a bronze winged figure of Peace.

This particular monument later had wreaths laid on it by the Prince of Wales, on 30th May, 1923, and by the Duke of York on 27th April, 1928.

The Skipton memorial is on a prominent site near the town centre, and close to Skipton Castle. A bronze winged figure of Victory stands on top of a very tall stone shaft, while at the foot is a very unusual and imaginative bronze of a warrior resting one knee on the ground, while he breaks his sword across the other. The memorial appears to have been recently cleaned and is

181   *The Skipton Memorial, Yorkshire*

182 *St. Anne's Memorial, Lancashire*

surrounded by attractive green and gold painted railings.

  The monument, which commemorates some 370 men of the town who died, was designed by John Cassidy of Manchester, and unveiled on 8th April, 1922.

182a *St. Anne's. A Bronze Panel*

A feature of the St. Anne's war memorial, in the borough of Lytham St. Anne's, is the quality of its three bronze figures by Walter Marsden, one surmounting a stone obelisk and one on each side of the plinth. The former is a classical figure with arms outstretched to the skies while the lower ones are a woman with a child, and a soldier, both seated.

183 *The Bushey Memorial, Hertfordshire*

  The Bushey memorial takes the form of the stone figure of a mourning woman, one hand raised to her face and the other holding a laurel wreath. The sculptor was William Reid Dick and the work is situated on a corner site at the head of a flight of eight steps, and surrounded by an attractive garden planted principally with heather. The only inscription is "1914–1918."

  The war memorial in the centre of the town of Galashiels in the Scottish Borders is a most unusual one in several respects.

  A massive clock tower has at its base the names of the fallen on a large bronze plaque.

182b
*St. Anne's. A
Bronze Panel*

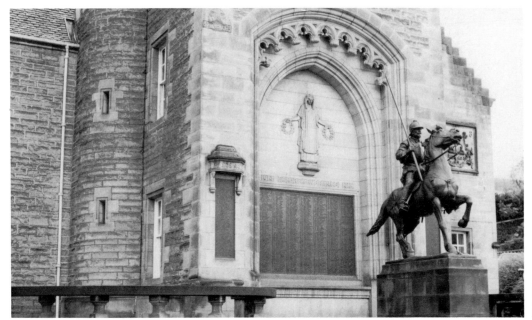

Above this, carved in stone, is a female figure with head bowed and holding a laurel wreath in each hand, and also in stone, the words
FOR REMEMBRANCE.

In front of the name plaque is a magnificent bronze equestrian statue, on a stone plinth, of a "Border Reiver" from Gala's earlier history.

Each evening a few bars of the *Braw, Braw Lads* is played in memory of the fallen after the chimes of the clock, and when at dusk the lighting is switched on, the shadows of what appear to be perfect wings are cast on to the female figure on the front of the memorial.

A plaque to one side of the tower refers to the laying of an inscribed stone in the presence of the Prince of Wales on 3rd December, 1924, and the unveiling ceremony by Field Marshal Earl Haig of Bemersyde on 4th October, 1925. The sculptor was Thomas J. Clapperton.

road. Designed by Wynyard Dixon, the tower was built on land donated by Mr. R. H. R. Rimington-Wilson and paid for by public subscription.

Plaques give the names of over 100 men who fell in the Great War, and that of one woman, Lucy Castledine, together with the inscription,
TO THE HONOUR AND EVERLASTING MEMORY OF THE SOLDIERS SAILORS AND NURSE OF THIS DISTRICT, WHO GAVE THEIR LIVES FOR THEIR KING AND COUNTRY IN THE GREAT WAR 1914-1918.

Early photographs show a long stairway, from the main road, reaching almost to the clock-tower and, half-way up, what appears to be a fountain. Nowadays the steps are limited in number and soon terminate in a stone wall. There is no sign at all of the fountain. Despite these changes the gardens and tower itself are well-kept and make an impressive tribute.

185   *The Stocksbridge Memorial, Yorkshire*

186   *The Senghenydd Memorial*

Another Clock Tower memorial is at Stocksbridge, near Sheffield, in attractive grounds on the side of the Sheffield-Manchester

The war memorial in Senghenydd, near Caerphilly, is also a clock tower. Surrounded by low railings, in a prominent position at a road

187   *The Scarborough Memorial*

188   *The Harrogate Memorial*

junction, it was financed by public subscription and unveiled on 1st March, 1921.

An unusual feature is that the names of the war memorial committee are recorded on a metal plaque on the base. Ironically, those names will soon be more legible than those of the 63 men who died in the war as their names, inscribed in stone, are beginning to show the effects of weathering.

The Scarborough memorial on top of Oliver's Mount, the highest point of the town and some 500ft. above sea level, is in the form of a 75ft. high obelisk surrounded by a platform and approached on each of the four sides by a flight of eleven steps. The obelisk is constructed of Yorkshire stone from the Crossland Moor Quarries and on the four sides of the base are bronze tablets recording the names of the fallen.

Over 700 men and women are commemorated by the monument and of these, 8 men, 9 women and 3 children were victims of the bombardments of the town in 1914 and 1917.

The memorial was designed by the Borough Engineer, Harry W. Smith, who acted as honorary architect, and built by J. Bastiman & Sons of Scarborough. It was unveiled on Wednesday, 26th September, 1923, by the Chairman of the War Memorial Committee, Councillor William Boyes, and dedicated by the Vicar of Scarborough, the Rev. J. Wynyard Capron.

Because of the distance from the town, a marquee was provided on Oliver's Mount so that the Mayor and Councillors could put on their official robes in the vicinity of the memorial.

Other obelisks include the Harrogate memorial erected on land formerly known as "Prospect Gardens", the garden of the Prospect Hotel, which the council had bought for road widening. The road schemes had been

completed and a suitable site in an open space remained.

The column was subsequently unveiled, on Saturday 1st September, 1923, by the Earl of Harewood, and dedicated by the Bishop of Ripon, Dr. T. B. Strong. Also present were Lady Harewood, Princess Mary and Viscount Lascelles.

Today surrounded by lawns and flower beds, on a prominent site in the town centre, the impressive memorial, designed by J. C. Prestwich and Sons of Leigh, is a 75ft. high structure on a base 16ft. square. On the north and south sides are bronze tablets listing the names of the 841 men and women from the town who died, and on the east and west are carved stone panels by Gilbert Ledward. The first panel represents "1914 — The Call to Arms", and the second "1918 — Britannia draped in The Flag holding out the Wreath of Victory" (see Plate C20, p.95).

Despite the inaccessibility of the site of the Saddleworth war memorial, on Pots and Pans hill in the Pennines east of Oldham, a large crowd attended the unveiling ceremony on Saturday, 6th October, 1923. One estimate was that almost 5,000 people climbed to the spot, 1,400ft. above sea level, on the edge of Saddleworth Moor.

The memorial was unveiled by Viscount Lascelles and dedicated by Canon Drury. To the left of a photograph taken at the ceremony can be seen, in uniform, the architect who designed the monument, Gilbert B. Howcroft. He served in the war, later writing a book about his war experiences, and is today in his mid-nineties.

His design was for a 52ft. high obelisk made of stone from the quarry near by. The cost of the monument which can be seen from miles

102

189   *The Saddleworth Memorial unveiling*

around, was £1,985 which would seem modest considering the difficulty of the site.

The names of 259 men from the area who died were inscribed on bronze plates at the base of the obelisk, the names of the men facing, as far as was possible, their former homes. In fact, the number killed represented one in fifty of the total population.

As part of the inscription on the memorial are the lines,

TRUE LOVE BY LIFE — TRUE LOVE BY DEATH IS TRIED,
LIVE THOU FOR ENGLAND — WE FOR ENGLAND DIED.

The Hyde war memorial, in honour of 710 men from the town who gave their lives in the war, was unveiled on Werneth Low on 25th June, 1921, when the deeds for the area were presented to Mayor Fawley. The column is on a commanding site overlooking the surrounding countryside for many miles, but despite the necessary climb a crowd in the region of 10,000 people attended the ceremony and a photograph and plan of the unveiling can be seen in the nearby Visitors' Centre jointly operated by the Civic Trust and the War Memorial Fund (see Plate C18, p.95).

190   *The Saddleworth Memorial*

Armistice Day, Saturday, 11th November, in 1922 was chosen for the unveiling by General Sir Hugh Ellis, of the war memorial at Corfe Castle, Dorset.

The memorial is in the form of a Tudor arch of Purbeck stone under a stone slate roof in an endeavour to reproduce the style of architecture common in old manor houses in the area of Corfe and the Isle of Purbeck. The arch forms an entrance to the cemetery, and the names of 34 men from the area are listed inside.

The arms of Corfe Castle and the County are to the side of the entrance above which an inscription stone bears the words,

DO'SET MEN DON'T SHEAME THEIR KIND,

191
*The Corfe
Castle
Memorial,
Dorset*

from the poem *In Praise of Dorset,* by William Barnes.

The design was by Professor Frances H. Newbury, Emeritus Director of the Glasgow School of Art.

Unfortunately, the original oak doors of antique design have subsequently been replaced by metal gates, and the dates 1914–1918 carved into the stone above the entrance were understandably removed when the Second War names were added to those of the First.

192 *The Broughton Memorial*

The Local History Group of Broughton, near Wrexham, recently donated the proceeds from a specially prepared magazine full of information about the two World Wars, towards a fund for restoring the local war memorial. The magazine's contents included reports of early meetings, to discuss possible schemes, and copies of the notices for those meetings, the first public meeting apparently being held on the 22nd January, 1919, although Parish Council discussions on the subject had started as early as 1917. In the event, the unveiling ceremony was on 19th November, 1923. The memorial took the form of gates leading into a recreation ground for the community's use. The gates themselves were described in the History Group's magazine as

"a pair of large, heavy central wrought-iron gates supported by two substantial decorated sandstone pillars on which are carved a wreath enclosing a date — one being 1914 and the other 1919. On the front faces of these pillars, white marble tablets have been attached and these carry the names of the seventy-six Broughton men who died in the Great War, in alphabetical order. On the left hand pillar above the tablets, the words THERE IS A LIFE IN DEATH are carved and on the right hand pillar YE HAVE NOT DIED IN VAIN. On either side of this central feature are hung pedestrian gates of similar design to those in the centre, and these are flanked by smaller sandstone pillars of similar design to the larger ones. Completing the layout, quadrant shaped low walls have been built onto which iron railings have been erected."

Although apparently without repair or maintenance for a very long time, the gates are now, as a result of the restoration, once again a fitting tribute to the fallen.

193 *The Rugby Memorial, immediately before re-siting*

Rugby war memorial also takes the form of wrought–iron gates, supported by two Portland stone piers with ornamental mountings. The names of the dead are engraved on the stone.

The memorial was designed by Mr. H. S. Goodhart-Rendel and unveiled on 12th March, 1922, by Field Marshal Earl French of Ypres, assisted by Mr. J. Hardman of Rugby, who lost three sons in the war. After the unveiling, the gates were dedicated by Dr. A. A. David, bishop of St. Edmundsbury and Ipswich, a former headmaster of Rugby School. The gates were then formally opened by Mr. Tom Reynolds of Rugby, another local man who had lost three sons in the war.

The original position of the memorial was at the main entrance to the Recreation Ground, but in 1987, for road improvement reasons, the gates were removed and resited further along the road.

The removal caused considerable controversy in the town and was approved by the town council only after the mayor had used her casting vote. A protest march through the town just before contractors moved in was supported by over 500 people. The £14,000 operation went ahead, however, and the Remembrance Service in November 1987 was held at the new site.

Although the gates no longer open onto the main route through the park, and indeed no longer lead anywhere, and although their new position means that they are to an extent hidden by trees, nevertheless they are now in a more peaceful spot and no longer at a road junction and near traffic lights, and most townspeople have found the move to be an improvement.

Many memorials have, over the years, been re-sited, mainly those in the centre of towns or

194
The Stratford-On-Avon Memorial (Photo by kind permission of the Shakespeare Birthplace Trust)

cities where traffic conditions have deteriorated and led to such a move. The memorial at Stratford is unusual in that it is now on its third site.

A photograph of the unveiling ceremony on Sunday, 12th February, 1922, shows the original position in the middle of the road in the town centre. This would appear to be a vulnerable spot and it subsequently proved to be so. In 1927 the memorial was struck by a lorry and the cross knocked from its plinth. It was decided, as a result, to resite the memorial and on 6th April, 1927 a committee met in the Bancroft Gardens, chose a new site there for the cross, and approved a tender of £60 from Messrs. Clifford & Sons to repair and re-erect it.

Finally, in 1954 it was moved again to a new Garden of Remembrance some little way from the centre of the town, but with beautiful flower beds and well-tended lawns and gravel paths.

Among the wooden benches in the Garden is one given

IN MEMORY OF A FATHER AND SON WHO GAVE THEIR LIVES.
ALFRED LEWIS ARNOLD, AUGUST 1917
BERTRAM LEWIS ARNOLD, OCTOBER 1944.

The original unveiling was, unusually, carried out jointly by three men, Lieut. Colonel Pepys, D.S.O., Sergeant Harry Smith, D.C.M., M.M., and Lance Sergeant Edward Townsend, Medal and Star of the 1882 Egyptian Campaign.

The Order of Service for the ceremony listed the names of 235 men of Stratford who laid down their lives in the war.

The unusual and attractive war memorial to be found in Bishop Auckland's Market Place was not, in fact, originally erected on that site. Early photographs show it in a position close to the railway station and development in that area has led to its re-siting. Often under similar circumstances the removal and re-erection of monuments has had unhappy results, but in this case the new location seems most appropriate and the memorial is in good repair and in a prominent position.

The war memorial at Haydon Bridge, Northumberland, was originally erected in 1921 on a site, on the main Newcastle-Carlisle road, which became increasingly inappropriate for the holding of Armistice Day services as years passed.

When, in the 60's, the building of a new bridge meant that an alternative site had to be found for the memorial, a much more suitable one was chosen next to the church and churchyard. The monument, a bronze statue of a soldier on a massive stone plinth, had been vandalised some years before when the bayonet had been taken from the soldier's rifle, and the opportunity was taken at the time of the re-erection to repair the damage.

To see the statue now, well maintained and in the shadow of the parish church, yet easily seen by passers-by, it is difficult to imagine that it had ever been sited elsewhere.

The construction of buildings such as hospitals or museums or art galleries, was more commonly undertaken by large towns or cities,

195   *The Bishop Auckland Memorial, Co. Durham*

196   *The Haydon Bridge Memorial, Northumberland*

although there are examples in smaller communities.

The High Wycombe memorial to over 500 dead, consisted of a cross in the churchyard of the Parish Church, and the High Wycombe and District War Memorial Hospital on Marlow Hill. The hospital was opened at 2.00 p.m. on Sunday, 9th December, 1923, by Field Marshal Sir William Robertson and dedicated by Bishop Shaw, and the Portland stone cross was unveiled by Sir William at 3.15 p.m., 15 minutes earlier than the advertised time due to the bitterly cold weather.

The hospital was built by Messrs. G. Biggs and Sons of High Wycombe, the contract price being £32,315 and the joint architects were Messrs. Cubitt of High Wycombe, and Marchment of London. Some three dozen beds were immediately provided and provision made in the construction for eventual expansion to 128 beds. The *Bucks Free Press* said, "It will be seen therefore that the requirements of not merely the immediate future, but of at least the remainder of the present century have been taken into account."

This unfortunately proved not to be the case. The old hospital was replaced by the present Wycombe General Hospital and when the third phase of this was started in 1971 the memorial plaques were removed to the entrance of the new hospital where they can be seen today. In addition to a descriptive plaque and the plaques carrying the names of the fallen, there is also a stone commemorating the unveiling, and the original foundation stone laid by the Marquis of Lincolnshire in 1922.

The red sandstone column in Central Park, South Gosforth, unveiled on 28th January, 1925, by the Duke of Northumberland, as part of Gosforth's war memorial, has a plaque on it referring to the other half of the memorial:

THIS COLUMN AND ADJACENT BUILDING WERE ERECTED BY PUBLIC SUBSCRIPTION TO THE MEMORY OF THE MEN OF GOSFORTH WHO FELL IN THE GREAT WAR 1914-18. THEIR NAMES ARE INSCRIBED ON A TABLET IN THE VESTIBULE OF THE BUILDING.

The building in question, on the edge of the park, is a Health Centre, and is an attractively designed and well-maintained property with a plaque on the gate referring to its origin.

In February 1919 a letter from Reginald Arthur Tatton to the mayor of Chorley in Lancashire, offered Astley Hall as a gift to the town to be used as part of its war memorial. The Hall, which had been in Tatton's family for over three centuries, together with a certain amount of its furniture, and the adjoining Astley Park, were conveyed to the town on 24th February, 1922.

198   *The Chorley Memorial, Lancashire*

Public subscriptions were used to convert the old 16th century mansion into a Museum and Art Gallery, to improve the Park and equip it for public use, to erect a monument in the style of Chorley Market Cross, and to build a stone wall and ornamental iron railings along the Park Road frontage, together with a Memorial Arch moved from elsewhere and rebuilt as the main entrance to Astley Park.

This most comprehensive of war memorials, made possible initially by one man's generosity, was opened officially on Saturday, 31st May, 1924.

The war memorial in Cottingham, near Hull, is in the form of a Memorial Club. The formal opening ceremony was held on 3rd July, 1920, and performed by Colonel B. G. Price who,

197
The Gosforth Memorial, Northumberland

during the war, had commanded the 150th Brigade, 50th Northumbrian Division.

In his speech he referred to the wonderful effort of the local people in completing such an ambitious scheme. A large number attended the ceremony and afterwards made a tour of the premises which had been so tastefully converted into a club.

This fine building certainly makes an impressive form of commemoration and, looking out over a small and attractive public park, still exists as a club.

The original named trustees of the Memorial Hall, which is Frome's war memorial to its 223 dead of the First World War, were replaced by the local Town Council under a deed of trust instituted by the Charity Commission in 1952. From this transfer may stem the uncertain future of the Hall.

It now seems possible that the Hall, because of the running and maintenance costs, may face closure and demolition when the present agency agreement with the Frome Amateur Operatic Society ends in October 1988.

The Hall, with a seating capacity of 600, was built by public subscription on gifted land with many special donations coming from local firms including mahogany entrance doors, and the bronze memorial tablets in the foyer. The Marquess of Bath laid an inscribed stone in September 1924, and the Hall was opened on Easter Monday, 13th April 1925, by General Sir Ian Hamilton. The architect was Percival B. Rigg.

The first use of the hall was to stage a Gilbert and Sullivan opera, *The Sorcerer,* performed by the Frome Operatic Society, and on 11th May, 1925, it was the venue for the Mid–Somerset Musical Festival, held outside Bath for the first time. The *Somerset Guardian* praised "the size and suitability of the Memorial Hall." Since then it has had a varied career as cinema, theatre, bingo hall, dance hall and public assembly hall.

Most towns would welcome such an attractive and versatile building and it is to be hoped that the townspeople of Frome and the Charity Commission are able to persuade the Frome Town Council to use its imagination and to overcome whatever difficulties of maintenance or use may appear temporarily, in order to ensure the Memorial Hall's existence, particularly in view of the original reason for its construction.

In his address at the opening of the Hall, Sir Ian Hamilton warned, "If you don't want another war memorial, you must keep a close watch on statesmen of whatever political party. If you do

not, then the suckling babes of Frome today, will, thirty years hence, be building new memorials to their small toddling brothers."

His warning showed remarkable foresight, but in addition, his mistrust of politicians shown by the speech would certainly have prompted a forthright comment on the present difficulties for the Memorial Hall which he opened.

In towns, as in villages, the wide variety of memorials makes categorizing extremely difficult.

When the population of Loughborough was asked to vote for their choice of war memorial on 6th November, 1919, they had three possibilities before them. The first was some form of conventional monument, the second was a health centre, and the third, most unusually, was a tower and carillon. With great enterprise and despite the high cost, they voted by a majority for the carillon (see Plate C21, p.95).

Claimed as the only Municipal Grand Carillon in Great Britain, its total cost was finally almost £20,000, an enormous sum for a town of Loughborough's size. A contract to build the bell-tower for £10,500 was placed with the local firm William Moss & Sons Limited, and the order for the carillon was placed with the well known local firm of founders John Taylor & Sons. The cost of the 47 bells was £7,000, towards which Messrs. Taylors themselves contributed £2,000. Eventually almost all of the bells were given by either individuals or local organisations.

The main tower is built of small 2 inch red bricks with a base of Portland stone. The upper part of the construction is of wood covered with copper and consists of a Main Gallery, a smaller octagonal gallery and a domed roof surmounted by a ball and golden cross. The total height of the tower to the top of the cross is 151ft. Almost all of the contracts, except for the copper work, were carried out by local firms using local labour.

The memorial was unveiled in Queens Park on Sunday, July 22nd, 1923 by Field Marshal Sir William Robertson, and the Bishop of Peterborough pronounced the dedication. On that day the carillon of 47 bells was first played by Chevalier Jef. Denyn of Malines, Belgium.

The total weight of the 47 bells is twenty-one tons, the largest being 82 cwts. and the smallest 20 lbs. The dimensions of the largest are 60ins. in height and 72ins. in diameter while the smallest is 7½ins. in height and 7ins. in diameter.

Inscriptions on the individual bells give information about the donors, and in some cases, men commemorated. The largest of the bells is inscribed

"In proud, loving memory of his three nephews, killed in action in France, John William Taylor, Courcelette, 1916; Gerard Bardsley Taylor, St. Quentin 1918, Arnold Bradley Taylor, Contalmaison 1916; sons of John William Taylor (1853-1919), grandsons of John William Taylor (1827-1906), Edmund Denison Taylor, the founder of these bells, gives this the largest, 1923."

Other inscriptions include the following —
"The gift of the Engineering and Allied Trades of Loughborough"
"The gift of the Building and Allied Trades of Loughborough" (the cost of trade bells was generally raised by small weekly contributions by men and women in these industries).
"The gift of the sons of William and Anne Moss, Third Mayor and Mayoress of this Borough, two of whose grandsons Howard James Harding Moss (2nd Lieut. 5th Leicesters) and Gerald Alec Moss (2nd Lieut. 2nd Manchesters) fell in the Great War."
"The gift of the Loughborough Grammar School (Past and Present) in memory of the 57 Old Boys who fell in the Great War."
"Given by Charles and Florence Wightman in memory of Lieut. John F. Wightman, R.A.F., killed in action 4th Sept. 1917, aged 18."
"The gift of Thomas Bowley Garton, M.C., in thankfulness for safe return."

201
The Stonehaven Memorial

108

202   *The Leighton Buzzard Memorial, Bedfordshire*   203   *The Beaconsfield Memorial, Buckinghamshire*

"The gift of Loughborough Corporation Workmen, in memory of F. Bishop, F. C. Fletcher, E. Grant."

"The gift of Old Comrades of the Church Lads' Brigade."

Names of all the fallen are, in fact, on bronze tablets on the stone base of the memorial.

The war memorial at Stonehaven near Aberdeen, stands high on a hill overlooking both the town and the sea.

A most unusual temple-like structure, open to the sky and with eight massive pillars, the memorial commands wonderful views, and conveys a very marked atmosphere of isolation and peace.

A flight of steps on one side leads up to a memorial stone, inscribed with the names of the dead and standing inside the monument. Carved outside are the names of some of the major actions of the war — Mons, Ypres, Vimy, Somme, Marne, Zeebrugge, Gallipoli and Jutland, and on the inside are the words:

ONE BY ONE DEATH CHALLENGED THEM. ONE BY ONE THEY SMILED IN HIS GRIM VISAGE AND REFUSED TO BE DISMAYED.

At Leighton Buzzard the largest block of granite ever quarried in the British Isles was used in 1920 to commemorate the 171 men killed in the war. The block was from the Shap quarries and the monolith, which stands in Church Square, is 25ft. 3ins. high by 3ft. 3ins. square. It weighs 22 tons and took 3 days to erect. Lord Ampthill unveiled the memorial on 11th November, 1920

in front of a crowd of some 5,000 people. Names from the Second World War and Korean War have been added since.

The Beaconsfield war memorial was erected in the Broadway close to the Parish Church. An imposing structure, it consists of a column 21ft. in height standing on a square base, surmounted by a lantern and with a crucifix in front, while inscribed on tablets at the base are the names of the 80 fallen out of a total of 489 local men who served in the war.

The monument was unveiled in May 1921 by Field Marshal Lord Grenfell whose nephew, it was said during the ceremony, fell gaining the first V.C. of the war. Prayers were said by the Right Rev. Bishop Shaw (Archdeacon of Oxford) who dedicated the memorial, and a touching reference was made to the great loss which Bishop Shaw had sustained in the death of his three sons, whose names in fact appear on the tablets.

The architect employed was J. Cheadle of Lincoln's Inn, and the contractors were Messrs. Wooldridge and Simpson of Oxford.

The following inscription appears on the memorial,

TO THE GLORIOUS MEMORY OF THE BRAVE AND TRUE, WHO GAVE THEIR LIVES IN THE GREAT WAR 1914-18. ETERNAL REST GRANT UNTO THEM O LORD; LET LIGHT PERPETUAL SHINE UPON THEM.

And indeed, today a light shines in the lantern which forms the top of the memorial, itself surrounded by an attractive and well tended garden.

109

The roadside war memorial at Castle Bromwich, near Birmingham, is in the form of an Altar of Remembrance. Of the thirty-three names of men killed in the First World War, three are of brothers, E., F., and G. Irons.

When the Guildford War Memorial Committee held a competition to help it choose a suitable design, Sir Edwin Lutyens, the designer of the Cenotaph in London, and himself a local man, acted as assessor. The first prize was £25 and the scheme was to cost about £1,500. A large number of designs were submitted and Lutyens awarded first place to that of Mr. Dening of Bristol for a memorial in the style of a cenotaph, but, although it secured the prize, the scheme was rejected by the committee.

Also, at that time, financial difficulties arose, as the amount of money received in response to a public appeal was less than £600, rather than the £1,500 anticipated.

Finally a design from a local architect, Mr. F. J. Hodgson, was adopted. This took the form of a colonnade raised on three steps and finished with urns symbolic of the ashes of the dead. On one side of each pillar a Sword of Honour and Wreath of Victory were carved while, on two other sides, panels of Portland stone were let into the surface to carry the inscription of the names of the 492

dead. It was realized at the time that bronze panels would be more durable, but cost was a problem, and indeed today the panels, and the memorial generally, show signs of weathering.

The site chosen for the memorial was an attractive one just inside the Castle grounds and facing the old bowling green, which, in fact, still exists today (see Plate C22, p.96).

The unveiling ceremony took place on Sunday, November 6th, 1921, in the presence of a crowd of some 5,000 people. Lieut.-General Sir Edmund Elles performed the ceremony, the Bishop of Winchester, Dr. E. S. Talbot, offered the dedicatory prayer and buglers of the Queen's sounded the *Last Post* and *Reveille*.

The original war memorial in Kettering, Northamptonshire, was a temporary wooden cenotaph outside the Kettering Library, and on 11th November, 1919, this was the scene for the march past of the Armistice Parade. Very soon afterwards, however, the people of the town erected a similar but permanent memorial of stone and this was unveiled in 1921.

A beautiful walled Garden of Remembrance in a park in Todmorden, Yorkshire, contains as its principal feature a war memorial fountain. The stone fountain, a decorated plinth surmounted by a figure of St. George, is the 1924 work of the

206   *The Todmorden Memorial, Yorkshire*

sculptor Gilbert Bayes.

On the wall behind it is a stone tablet inscribed,

THESE ARE THEY WHO BEING PEACABLE CITIZENS OF
TODMORDEN, AT THE CALL OF KING AND COUNTRY
AND IN DEFENCE OF THEIR NATIVE LAND, LEFT ALL
THAT WAS DEAR TO THEM, ENDURED HARDSHIP
FACED DANGER AND FINALLY PASSED OUT OF SIGHT
OF MAN BY THE PATH OF DUTY AND SELF-SACRIFICE,
GIVING UP THEIR OWN LIVES THAT OTHERS MIGHT
LIVE IN FREEDOM.

On the walls which stretch on either side of the fountain are stone plaques with the names of almost 700 of the fallen, while in front of the fountain, and framing the view of it from the main entrance to the garden, are two stone statues representing, on one side, the Lamp of Memory and on the other, the Shield of Honour. The rest of the garden is laid out with immaculate lawns and flower beds.

On the sea-front at Hartlepool is a memorial tablet marking the place where the first shell from a German warship struck on 16th December, 1914, and where the first soldier was killed by enemy action on British soil during the war.

Many civilians were killed during such coastal bombardment and the effect on the morale of a nation which had such confidence in its navy must initially have been considerable.

On the same day as the bombardment of Hartlepool, similar attacks were carried out further down the coast on Whitby and Scarborough.

The memorial in the Shrewsbury park known as the Quarry is, in fact, part of the Shropshire War Memorial which altogether comprised a monument, a Roll of Honour placed in the Shrewsbury Museum, £9,000 given to the Royal Shropshire Infirmary, and a similar figure to the Shropshire Orthopaedic Hospital.

The monument in the Quarry, close to St. Chad's Church, is in design a classic temple with six columns supporting a shallow dome. On the floor are carved the arms of the county and of the Borough of Shrewsbury, the Croix de Guerre, the badge of the King's Shropshire Light Infantry, a cross, and the inscription

REMEMBER THE GALLANT MEN OF SHROPSHIRE WHO
FOUGHT FOR GOD, KING AND COUNTRY 1914-1918.

In the centre is a bronze statue of St. Michael with a lance in his left hand, and his right arm extended in benediction. The sculptor was Allan G. Wyon and the architect was George Hubbard, who had designed the base of the Cambridgeshire memorial. The unveiling in July 1922 was by the Lord Lieutenant of the County, Lord Powis.

The Roll of Honour when compiled included the names of 5,581 men from 240 parishes: 326 names were from Shrewsbury School.

Inside the Church of St. Peter and St. Paul in the lovely Suffolk town of Lavenham is a

207
The
Shrewsbury
Memorial

beautiful stone wall plaque with attractive carvings, and the names of 76 men of the town inscribed in gold lettering. In addition to this plaque, these men who fell in the Great War are also commemorated in a more unusual way.

On a side table under the memorial is a book containing a short biography of each of the Lavenham men who died, these biographies having been written by the then Rector.

As the first page of the book explains,
"This book has been compiled that something, more than their mere names, may be known of the Lavenham men who gave their lives for their Country in the Great War.
Signed by G. H. Lenox Conyngham.
Rector of Lavenham 1922."

Amongst the entries is one about Frederick Thomas Smith of the Royal Army Medical Corps who was killed in action on November 18th, 1916. His Chaplain wrote
"Your boy died while performing the merciful work of rescuing the wounded. In the great sorrow which has come to you it will be a pride to you that he died as a soldier, doing a brave thing."

Two Wheeler brothers of 1 High Street, Lavenham, were killed out of a total of six brothers who joined the army.

Frank Wheeler had emigrated to Canada and joined the army there. He trained with the 75th Canadians, went to France in November 1916 and was killed on January 1st, 1917 by a shell which killed nine of a party of thirteen men. The entry goes on,
"His friend who was unhurt went to him and said, 'Are you hurt Frank?' The answer was,

'They've got me this time.' His friend took off Frank's knap-sack and put it under his head, went and did the same for another man, then came back to Frank who asked how soon the ambulance would come, and died just as he was speaking."
His brother Frederick was killed on 17th June, 1917, having enlisted in the Royal Fusiliers in 1915.
"A shell came over and burst in the very shell hole where he was, and blew him to pieces. He left a wife and three children."

The entry for George Twitchett of Water Street is as follows,
"Was in Territorials. Called up on August 4th, 1914. Trained at Watford. Landed in Gallipoli at Suvla Bay. Reported missing August 15th 1915. His mother died brokenhearted within three weeks of hearing of her son's death."

After the Second World War similar biographies were written by the Rector at that time, for those of the town who died in action during those years.

The book is a wonderful idea and leaves an impression which the memorial alone cannot do. However, because it is so readily available to the public its pages are becoming rather dog-eared and one or two small pieces of graffiti appear in it, and it might now be wiser to enclose it in a glass case to which access could be allowed by whoever is manning the bookstall in the church. The church seems to have someone regularly in attendance and similar arrangements are normally made for Rolls of Honour in churches, often the pages being turned daily by those in charge.

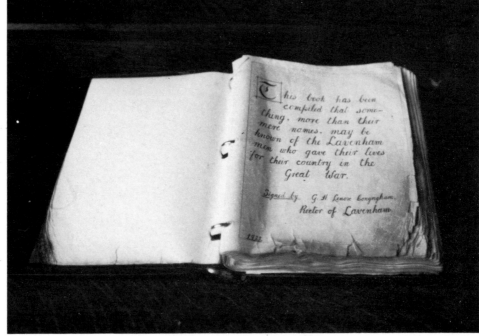

208 *The Lavenham Memorial, Suffolk*

C26   *The Rochdale Memorial*

C27   *The Bedford Memorial*

C28   *The Lancaster Memorial*

The Scottish National War Memorial
C29   Top: *The Memorial Front*   C30   Right: *St. Michael*
C31   Above: *Part of the Hall of Honour*
       (Photographs by kind permission of the Trustees of the
       Scottish National War Memorial)

C32   *The Cenotaph. Principal Wreaths Laid, Remembrance Day 1987*

114

Chapter VII

Large Towns and Cities

In the larger towns and cities, with their greater resources, it was common for the war memorial to take the form of a hospital, or art gallery, or museum, or some similar building requiring extensive financial support.

Often those cities which planned hospitals also included a more conventional monument as part of the scheme. Examples of such comprehensive memorials can be found in Portsmouth, Ipswich, Darlington, London, Colchester and Huddersfield, while Derby and Newcastle had more limited schemes.

The appeal by the Mayor of Portsmouth, John Timpson, in a letter to *The Hampshire Telegraph & Post* on 27th December, 1918, was both for suggestions as to the type of war memorial which the city should have, and for donations towards a memorial fund.

Eventually almost £30,000 was received, £10,000 of which was allocated as a gift to the Royal Portsmouth Hospital, the balance being set aside for a suitable monument. The design for this was thrown open to competition and from no fewer than 50 designs sent in, an assessor appointed by the British Association of Architects chose that of Messrs. Gibson & Gordon of Old Bond Street, London.

Their design consisted of a central raised cenotaph behind which was a semi-circular 22ft. high wall carrying ten name panels, five for the army and five for the navy, and in front of which were two pedestals with pieces of statuary representing respectively the army and the navy. The memorial was basically of Portland stone and the site on which it was erected adjoined the Guildhall.

A crowd estimated to be almost 30,000 strong attended the unveiling ceremony by the Duke of Connaught on 19th October, 1921.

Of the £10,000 given to the Royal Portsmouth Hospital from the City's war memorial fund, the bulk went into improvements and additions within the hospital, but part was used to improve the entrance to the hospital and to build a new War Memorial Gateway on Commercial Road.

The gateway, opened officially by Princess Helena Victoria on 19th May, 1922, unfortunately no longer exists having been demolished comparatively recently, along with the hospital itself, in a major redevelopment of the area.

When the type of memorial that Portsmouth should have, was being discussed, the view was put forward forcibly that money spent on the

209
The Portsmouth Memorial

210 *The Portsmouth Memorial*

211 *Portsmouth, a detail from the column*

Cenotaph, or other monument, was wasted and that money spent on a hospital was better used, but in the long run the memorial in Portsmouth still remains as a tribute to the dead, while the improved hospital has ceased to exist.

The Ipswich cenotaph, in a prominent position in Christchurch Park, was unveiled on Saturday, May 3rd, 1924. The programme of proceedings listed 1,481 names recorded on the memorial and these names are on bronze tablets on a wall behind the main column.

In front is a large bronze trophy of arms described in the programme as

"Symbolizing the accoutrements of the war laid aside. It is built up of equipment, including regimental standards, bundles of lances, machine guns and Stokes trench gun with tripod and shells. The whole is bound together with cords and draped with the Union Jack and St. George's banner.

In the centre is depicted the personal equipment of the soldier — haversack, trenching tool, water bottle and gas mask, interwoven with stems of oak and laurel and surmounted by a rifle and helmet."

In addition to this monument a new wing to the East Suffolk and Ipswich Hospital was built as a memorial. The original plans for the wing show it projecting from the centre of the existing building, with three wards, and the necessary kitchens, stores and offices, all at an estimated cost of £50,000.

This wing still exists today but unfortunately is no longer in use. This large and impressive building lies empty while erected in front of it, destroying any overall view of the main elevation, is a series of wooden huts which are themselves in use. Quite apart from any sentiment about the building as a war memorial, it is difficult to believe that heating or maintenance costs can condemn such a structure as useless for very long, while encouraging the erection and occupation of unsightly shacks.

The Ipswich authorities, health or municipal, must be very fortunate in their facilities elsewhere to be unable to find some valuable use, medical, leisure or commercial, for their war memorial building which must surely deteriorate if not occupied.

On the wall of the memorial wing is an elaborate plaque which can now be seen only with difficulty, except from very close, because of the wooden buildings.

On it is inscribed,
IPSWICH WAR MEMORIAL WING.
ERECTED BY PUBLIC SUBSCRIPTION IN GRATEFUL MEMORY OF THE MEN OF IPSWICH WHO GAVE THEIR LIVES FOR THEIR COUNTRY IN THE GREAT WAR 1914-1918.

Darlington's tribute to its 700 dead is in the form of a Memorial Hospital, and, in the grounds in front of it, a simple obelisk of Stainton stone on a two-tiered base.

The foundation stone of the hospital is dated 1926 and soon after the building's completion,

212
*Ipswich
Hospital
Memorial
Wing*

116

213
The Darlington Memorial

the memorial column was unveiled, at 3.00 p.m. on Sunday, 11th November, 1928. An ex-serviceman, ex-sergeant in the Durham Light Infantry, Joseph Stephenson, who had been chosen by ballot, unveiled the memorial in front of a crowd of some 9,000 people.

He had not known of the honour until minutes before the ceremony. Twenty-five men provided by the Darlington British Legion had assembled in the Hospital's Hall of Remembrance and once the ballot was completed the other twenty-four accompanied Stephenson as a guard of honour during the unveiling.

The dedication prayers were read by the Vicar of Darlington, the Reverend R. F. Drury, and at the end of the service the public were invited to inspect the Administration Block of the new memorial hospital.

The major Islington war memorial is the Casualty Department of the Royal Northern Hospital in Holloway Road, together with a memorial arch listing the 1,337 Islington dead. This archway became the entrance for patients to all departments of the hospital.

The foundation stone of the new extension to the hospital was laid by Lady Patricia Ramsey in July 1923 and work on the building went ahead so quickly, that the official opening of the department was performed by the Prince of Wales on 27th November, 1923.

A wall plaque on the building reads,
BOROUGH OF ISLINGTON WAR MEMORIAL
THIS BUILDING WAS ERECTED BY PUBLIC
SUBSCRIPTION RAISED IN THE BOROUGH OF
ISLINGTON TO COMMEMORATE THE SUPREME
SACRIFICE MADE BY THOSE WHO FELL IN THE GREAT
WAR AND THE BRAVE DEEDS OF THOSE WHO WERE
SPARED. 1914-1919.

The St. Marylebone war memorial in Park Road, N.W.8. was, in fact, a gift to the borough by the artist Sigismund Goetze. His bronze statue of St. George slaying the dragon was not unveiled until April 1936. After the war, the War Memorial Committee had concentrated its efforts on providing a War Memorial Ward in Middlesex Hospital and these efforts had culminated in a Service of Dedication conducted by the Bishop of Willesden on 3rd November, 1920, at the completion of the scheme.

At the end of the 1914-18 war a hospital was built in Midland Road, Peterborough as a memorial to more than 1,000 of the area who died in the war. It was opened by Prince George and a plaque in the entrance to the building states —
THIS HOSPITAL WAS ERECTED IN 1928 AT A COST OF
£90,000 BY PUBLIC SUBSCRIPTION FROM
PETERBOROUGH AND DISTRICT AS A WAR MEMORIAL
UPON THIS SITE WHICH WAS GENEROUSLY GIVEN BY
ALDERMAN J. H. BUNTING AT A COST OF £5,500.

The architect is named as Wallace Marchment and the Builder as Robert S. Jellings. Special donations to the building fund included £10,000 from the Peterborough hospital fund, £10,769 from the local Red Cross Committee and £3,000 from the British Red Cross.

After the Second World War the hospital became also a memorial to the dead of 1939-1945 and on Remembrance Days wreaths were laid in the main entrance.

However, after the National Health Authorities took over the management, a new building was added and the whole became the Peterborough and District Hospital and gradually it was felt that the original concept as a War Memorial was lost.

Eventually a committee was formed to plan a

214   *The St Marylebone Memorial*

new memorial in the town centre and these plans finally came to fruition on 2nd November, 1986 when a monument in Bridge Street was unveiled by Princess Alice and dedicated by the Bishop of Peterborough. The monument is in the form of a solid cube of Weldon stone 8ft. x 8ft. x 8ft. on a four-step plinth. On one side is engraved Laurence Binyon's verse *For the Fallen* — "They shall grow not old . . .", and on the opposite side, the words of the Kohimar Epitaph. On the other two sides are engraved wreaths of poppies.

The total cost of the new memorial was in the region of £30,000, some £26,000 of which was still to be raised at the time of the unveiling, according to statements in the *Peterborough Standard* which also reported some criticism of the shape and design of the memorial. Whatever those arguments it is difficult not to admire the persistence of the ex-servicemen who pursued their aim, over so many years, of having a Peterborough war memorial which is clearly identifiable and accessible. A veteran of Ypres and the Somme and holder of the Military Medal, wrote in a letter to the *Standard,* "I hope the discordants will change their minds and be thankful we now have a suitable symbol of remembrance of the sacrifice made on our behalf in the Two World Wars" (see Plate C23, p.96).

At a town meeting held in Acton in 1918 it was decided that the chief local war memorial should be the enlargement of the hospital in Gunnersbury Lane, and the fruition of this scheme came some five years later.

The hospital extension which had cost over £20,000, was opened on 12th July, 1923, by the Rt. Hon. A. Neville Chamberlain, then Minister of Health and later Prime Minister.

Early in his speech the minister said, "I am not so ignorant about hospitals as you would naturally expect a Minister of Health to be," and then went on to praise the new facilities and those who had worked for them, including the architect, Mr. C. H. Monson.

A memorial tablet unveiled by Mr. Chamberlain was at that time over the entrance to the out-patients' department and is now inside the building.

It is inscribed,
THIS OUT-PATIENTS' DEPARTMENT AND THE TWO WARDS AT THE SOUTHERN END OF THIS HOSPITAL WERE ERECTED BY THE PEOPLE OF ACTON 1922-23 AS A MEMORIAL OF THOSE MEN AND WOMEN OF ACTON WHO LOST THEIR LIVES IN THE GREAT WAR 1914-18. THEIR NAMES ARE INSCRIBED IN A BOOK WHICH CAN BE SEEN AT THE COUNCIL OFFICES.

Contemporary reports gave the number of names in the Roll of Honour as over 750.

It is to be hoped that, whatever changes in the National Health Service lie ahead, the future of the Acton Hospital, a war memorial, will be secure.

The hospital on Shooter's Hill, which was Woolwich's war memorial to the 6,000 local men who died in the Great War, cost over £200,000 to build.

Woolwich, with its extensive military connections, raised the huge sum of £179,000 by local subscription, and, in order that the hospital could be opened free of debt on 2nd November 1927, a grant of £30,000 was made by the Borough Council just before that date.

The land for the War Memorial Hospital, which replaced the Woolwich and Plumstead Cottage Hospital, had been purchased in 1919, and the first turf was cut in February 1923 on Telegraph Field, which had been the site of a semaphore station during the Napoleonic Wars. In July 1925 the Duke of Connaught who was President of the Memorial Hospital Scheme, laid the Foundation Stone and on 2nd November, 1927, the hospital was opened by the Duke of York, later George VI, accompanied by Elizabeth, Duchess of York.

When George V visited the hospital on 27th March, 1928, he stated, "This is the best equipped and most beautiful hospital I have ever seen."

It is still, today, a very attractive building, on an elevated site and in well-tended grounds. In the heart of the building is the impressive Hall of Remembrance, panelled in different coloured marbles from Derbyshire, Cornwall, Sicily, Norway, Denmark and Italy. The marble figures of two angels hold a laurel wreath within which is the inscription,
THEY PASSED OUT OF THE SIGHT OF MEN BY THE PATH OF DUTY AND SELF-SACRIFICE.

215
The War Memorial Hospital, Woolwich

A beautifully bound and illuminated book contains the names of 6,320 local people of whom 100 or so had died in munition explosions at the Arsenal, and 14 had been killed by enemy air-raids. The casket containing the book was the gift of Mr. G. E. Dixon, O.B.E., J.P., in memory of his brother, Major G. S. Dixon, M.C. A second book was placed after the 1939-45 war, and pages of the books are turned each morning.

On each side hang flags representing the Army, Navy, R.A.F. and Merchant Navy, and let into the marble floor is the word SILENCE, a reminder observed in the area to this day (see Plate C24, p.96).

Once again, it is to be hoped that the future of the War Memorial Hospital is safe whatever changes in the National Health Service occur.

An example of a different type of war memorial building is the Stockport War Memorial and Art Gallery, built on the site of the old Stockport Grammar School in a prominent and elevated position at the junction of two main roads. The building, which was unveiled by Prince Henry on 15th October, 1925, was designed by Messrs. Halliday and Agate, and the total cost was raised by voluntary subscription.

Inside the building, the Memorial Hall itself has panels of white marble containing the names of some 2,300 dead, and the same material has been used for a memorial sculpture by Gilbert Ledward.

On each side of the entrance hall of the building is a small exhibition gallery, and on the first floor is the main gallery, from the entrance to which it is possible to look down into the impressive Memorial Hall or upwards to the dome (see Plate C25, p.96).

Plans for Aberdeen's war memorial, despite the scope and complexity of the scheme, were published in great detail as early as August 1919 when the *Aberdeen Daily Journal* explained the proposed lay-out and anticipated financial requirements. In fact, from that time until the scheme's fruition, there was little change to the details published.

The whole development consisted of a Memorial Court or Hall of Remembrance, an extension to the city's art gallery, a large hall and an art museum. The architects were Dr. A. Marshall Mackenzie, who was the architect of the original Art Gallery building, and A. G. R. Mackenzie.

Facing Union Terrace Gardens, the exterior of the Memorial Court was of concave shape, with six Corinthian pillars on a raised platform, in front of a wall upon which were carved a wreath of laurels, the arms of the city and county, the dates 1914-1919 in Roman numerals and the words

TO OUR GLORIOUS DEAD.

In front, in the centre of the crescent, was a lion modelled by William MacMillan, and on either side of the pillared wall was a handsome pier, each with an entrance door, one to the Memorial Court and one to the new hall and museum. The whole of the striking exterior was built of white granite.

The Memorial Court itself was circular, rising almost 80ft. to the top of a dome above. A hall large enough to accommodate 700 people was designed above an art museum, and other rooms served as extensions to the original art gallery.

The whole scheme cost in the region of £70,000. The site for the buildings cost the Corporation £7,000; £21,000 was subscribed by the public towards the war memorial; of the £12,000 contributed to the art gallery extensions, the sum of £7,000 came from the Clark Trustees; and Lord and Lady Cowdray generously offered to provide the Hall and Art Museum at a cost of £20,000, together with an organ for the hall.

A marble tablet bearing the sculptured Cowdray coat-of-arms, carried the inscription,

THE COWDRAY HALL AND ART MUSEUM WERE PRESENTED TO THE CITY BY VISCOUNT AND VISCOUNTESS COWDRAY FOR THE ADVANCEMENT OF LEARNING AND THE ENCOURAGEMENT OF ART AND MUSIC AMONG THE CITIZENS OF ABERDEEN, 1925.

The new buildings were opened by King George V on 29th September, 1925 and the war memorial was dedicated by the Moderators of the

216
The Aberdeen Memorial

119

Church of Scotland and the United Free Church of Scotland.

The Gordon Highlanders provided the King's guard of honour, and amongst the people to whom the King spoke was Captain Albert Hutcheon, M.C., who was blinded leading a company of the 5th Gordon Highlanders.

The Roll of Honour inside the Memorial Court contained 5,042 names — 535 officers, 4,505 other ranks and 2 women, a nurse and a medical missionary.

Four V.C.'s were listed, Captain James A. O. Brooke of the Gordon Highlanders, Lieut. Robert G. Combe of the Canadian Infantry, Captain Archibald B. Smith of the Royal Naval Reserve, and Brigadier Frederick W. Lumsden of the Royal Marine Artillery, who won not only the V.C. but the D.S.O. and three bars, believed to be a record for the British army. Captain Brooke was one of three brothers whose names were on the roll, and a brother-in-law also fell. There were several instances of four members of a family being listed and one family lost five sons.

The father of that family, Peter Tocher, formally placed the Roll of Honour in the casket on the shrine of the Memorial Court. He had lost one son, George, on the Menin Road near Ypres in 1915, three sons, Robert, John and James on the Somme in 1916, and one, Peter, after the war, his health undermined by four years as a prisoner of war. All five men were Gordon Highlanders, and their father also joined the regiment despite being 50 years old, but because of his age was not passed for active service.

The Birmingham Hall of Memory is a massive octagonal structure in Roman Doric style, 35ft. wide and standing at one end of a garden of lawns and flower beds, terminating in a colonnade.

The Hall, on a base of Cornish granite, is of Portland stone with a domed roof. The huge doors are of bronze and four bronze figures, representing the Army, Navy, Air Force and Women's Services, are on granite pedestals at the corners of the building.

In the interior a sarcophagus-shaped marble shrine supports the glass and bronze casket containing the Roll of Honour. The frontispiece of the Roll is a richly coloured and gilt border framing the words,
THERE WAS NONE THAT GAVE THEM AN ILL WORD, FOR THEY FEARED GOD GREATLY. SO THEY PASSED OVER, AND ALL THE TRUMPETS SOUNDED FOR THEM ON THE OTHER SIDE.

A stained-glass window showing the Cross faces the main entrance and on the walls are three bas-reliefs, illustrating episodes of the war. The first shows men leaving home for the war. The second shows them in the firing line with the inscription
AT THE GOING DOWN OF THE SUN AND IN THE MORNING WE WILL REMEMBER THEM.

The third shows men returning home, wounded and maimed.

The artists involved in the work were Albert Toft the sculptor of the bronze statues, Sidney Meteyard the designer of the Roll of Honour, William Bloye the designer of the bas-reliefs, R. J. Stubington the designer of the glass work, and the architects S. N. Cooke and W. N. Twist who were both ex-servicemen. Sir Reginald Blomfield had chosen the design after assessing those submitted.

One hundred and fifty thousand men and women of Birmingham had served in the war and of these 12,320 were killed and 35,000 wounded. Lists of names to be included in the Roll had remained open for weeks in case of necessary amendment, and the numbers of names to be included had increased considerably during that time.

The cost of the Hall was over £60,000, all from public subscription, and excluding the cost of the land which was given by the Corporation.

The foundation stone of the Hall of Memory was laid by the Prince of Wales on 12th June, 1923, and the Hall was opened by Prince Arthur of

218 *The Southampton Memorial*

Connaught on 4th July, 1925, when it was dedicated by the Bishop of Birmingham.

The Hall is a most impressive and appropriate memorial to the thousands of Birmingham war dead, and the building and gardens are well maintained. Unfortunately the colonnade is rather untidy and not free from graffiti. It is also unfortunate that the Hall cannot be manned during daytime hours, and that it is necessary to have to seek out the appropriate official in the City Hall in order to gain access.

Another large group of memorials were those influenced by the Cenotaph in Whitehall, and by the work of its architect, Sir Edwin Lutyens.

Southampton's Cenotaph was designed by Lutyens who was consulted by the city's war memorial committee as early as January 1919, and his eventual design for Southampton, with some modification, later became the basis for the design of the Cenotaph in Whitehall.

Lutyens' original brief was for a memorial at a cost not exceeding £10,000, and his first scheme, for a pair of archways to the entrances to East and West Park, proved to be too costly and was replaced by the present design and built on a site at the eastern entrance to West Park.

The memorial booklet describes the memorial as follows:

"Here, facing west is the Great War Stone of Remembrance, a monolith, an altar in form, identical to those which lie in each of our War Cemeteries throughout the War area, with the words chosen by Mr. Rudyard Kipling — Their name liveth for evermore — cut on its west face. Behind this stone, on a plinth, standing on a platform of steps, rises a great pylon.

On the north, south and west faces of this pylon, recessed in panels, are inscribed the 1,800 names of those who fell in the Great War. The panels being recessed, and the stones that built them being on their natural bed, the inscription is permanent.

The east side, facing the main road, contains a Great Cross, and on its surface is carved a sword crosswise. On the plinth is carved a Wreath of Victory. The pylon is surmounted by a cenotaph, supported north and south by lions and east and west by the Arms of Southampton.

On the cenotaph is placed a recumbent effigy of a fighting man. In that the effigy is placed high up, the face is not to be seen, so that in imagination it represents to every mother her son. The wreaths upon the cenotaph enclose emblems of the Army and Navy, including the Mercantile Marine, and Air Force, represented by the Anchor and the Royal Cypher.

Flanking the Monument are piers terminated with fir cones, emblems of eternity, joined by a wall and seat, and the words Our Glorious Dead are inscribed on the wall.

The whole of the Memorial is built of specially selected Portland stone, the best stone in England for durability, and weathering to a beautiful colour, growing whiter with age and retaining the character of the design."

The number of names inscribed on the memorial eventually increased to 2,008, as the committee continued to advertise for a further 6 months to make sure that no names were omitted, but unfortunately the engraving is now beginning to show signs of wear and work will be necessary, eventually, to preserve it.

The unveiling ceremony was held on 6th November, 1920, the unveiling being carried out by the Lord Lieutenant, Major-General Seeley

219 *Norwich, the Memorial on its original site*

121

and the dedication by the Bishop of Winchester, the Right Reverend Edward Stuart.

Another design by Lutyens was that for Norwich.

The Norwich War Memorial, which now stands in front of the City Hall, was originally placed in front of the east wall of the 15th century Guildhall, and it was there that it was unveiled on Sunday, 8th October, 1927.

Lutyens had chosen the Guildhall site from several suggested. His memorial incorporated both a Stone of Remembrance, similar to that placed in the War Cemeteries, with the inscription that had been chosen by Rudyard Kipling

THEIR NAME LIVETH FOR EVERMORE

and a Cenotaph under which was engraved

OUR GLORIOUS DEAD

and, in this case, bearing the City Arms of Norwich.

221   *Northampton's temporary cenotaph*

The unveiling ceremony was performed by an ex-serviceman chosen by lot, a disabled ex-private B. A. Withers, fittingly of the city's own battalion, the 1/4th Norfolks.

He was introduced, before the unveiling, to a crowd of over 40,000 by General Sir Ian Hamilton under whom, coincidentally, he had served in Gallipoli.

Reference was made in speeches during the ceremony to the fact that by 1927 most cities already had their war memorial.

By 1927 tentative schemes for a new City Hall were already under discussion and these came to fruition in 1938 when the present building was completed.

A Garden of Remembrance was laid out in front of the new City Hall and on 17th October, 1938 the memorial was moved to this new site overlooking the market.

In 1919 a temporary wooden cenotaph in Abington Street, Northampton, served a focal point for the ceremony commemorating the first anniversary of the war's end and the memory of the men who had died. This use of temporary memorials was common and in 1919 this was the case even in Whitehall.

In 1926 a permanent monument designed by Lutyens was unveiled in the city centre and the following year, on 7th July, 1927, a wreath was laid by the Prince of Wales.

To Lutyens' memorial of a Stone of

222   *The Prince of Wales laying a wreath at Northampton*

Remembrance flanked by two obelisks, was added, in 1937, a Garden of Remembrance in Abington Square. The main features of the garden are a wall recording the names of the fallen, and the Mobbs memorial moved from its original site.

The Manchester war memorial in St. Peter's Square, was unveiled on 12th July, 1924, by the

224　　*The Manchester Memorial*

Earl of Derby, assisted by a Mrs. Bingle of Ardwick, Manchester, whose three sons had been killed in the war.

The dedication of the memorial was by the Dean of Manchester, the Very Reverend J. G. McCormick.

There had been a great deal of discussion and controversy before a final choice of site. A letter dated 11th April, 1923, from the British Legion in Manchester, had come down emphatically in favour of Albert Square as the site of the memorial, but letters from the Manchester Society of Architects, the Manchester Art Federation, and the Royal Manchester Institution had all expressed opposition to such a scheme.

The memorial, finally built in St. Peter's Square, was designed by Sir Edwin Lutyens and covers an area of about 93ft. by 53ft. on the site of the foundations of St. Peter's Church.

The main feature is a pylon of Portland stone, 32ft. high and surmounted by a bier on which lies the body of a soldier covered by his greatcoat.

225
*The Glasgow
Memorial*

Before the pylon is a War Stone with the familiar inscription,

THEIR NAME LIVETH FOR EVERMORE,

and on either side is a 23ft. high stone obelisk.

Another impressive memorial is that in the centre of Rochdale, close to the Town Hall and Post Office buildings (see Plate C26, p.113).

The massive stone cenotaph with its war stone, elegant steps and service flags, is itself perfectly maintained and in an equally immaculate area of lawns, trees and flower tubs.

On the side of the monument is the inscription

THEY WERE A WALL UNTO US BOTH BY NIGHT AND BY DAY.

Glasgow's war memorial stands in the centre of the city, in George Square, with the City Chambers in the background. A massive Cenotaph and Stone of Remembrance flanked by two imposing lions, the memorial is the work of Sir John Burnet, and was unveiled on Saturday, 31st May, 1924, by Field Marshal Earl Haig.

On the back of the main column is the following interesting inscription,

TOTAL OF HIS MAJESTY'S FORCES ENGAGED AT HOME AND ABROAD 8,654,465. OF THIS NUMBER THE CITY OF GLASGOW RAISED OVER 200,000.

A photograph taken on 30th October, 1920, at the unveiling ceremony of Swindon's war memorial near the Town Hall, shows the monument itself just as it is today, with its clean uncomplicated lines and its recessed cross with the superimposed sword.

The buildings in the background of the photograph have now gone, however, and have been replaced by a modern shopping development. Attractive trees, part of that development, now flank the memorial without masking it.

An earlier photograph showed a temporary wooden cenotaph outside the General Post Office in Swindon. As we have mentioned, this form of temporary memorial existed in many

226   *The Swindon Memorial*

towns before their permanent monuments were erected.

The Belfast War Memorial was unveiled on Armistice Day, 11th November, 1929, by Field Marshal Lord Allenby, a former Inniskilling Dragoon, who had joined the famous regiment in 1882 and served in it for twenty years.

The dedicatory prayer was offered by the Bishop of Down and Connor and Dromore, the Right Rev. Dr. Grierson.

The memorial was built in a Garden of Remembrance on the west side of the City Hall, and took the form of a 30ft. high Cenotaph with the background of a 25ft. high curved colonnade.

Part of the inscription on the monument reads,

THROUGHOUT THE LONG YEARS OF STRUGGLE WHICH HAVE NOW SO GLORIOUSLY ENDED, THE MEN OF ULSTER HAVE PROVED HOW NOBLY THEY FIGHT AND DIE — GEORGE R.

The foundation stone of the sea-front war memorial at Swansea was laid on the 1st July, 1922, by Field Marshal Earl Haig, and the stone is engraved to that effect. Also engraved are the words,

UNDER THIS STONE LIES THE KING'S SHILLING, PLACED BY MRS. FEWINGS REPRESENTING THE WAR WIDOWS.

227
The Belfast Memorial (Photograph — Messrs. Anderson and McMeekin)

228
The Swansea Memorial

Mrs. Gertrude Fewings' name had been drawn out of a hat, and when she was told tactlessly by a reporter that she was the "lucky" one to be selected, the widowed mother of five apparently replied "Is it luck, I wonder?"

More than £9,000 had been subscribed to the war memorial fund, of which some £3,000 was donated to the Memorial Assistance Scheme to assist the children of men who had lost their lives. Over 15,000 men had volunteered for service from the city, and one in six had died.

The 30ft. high Portland stone Cenotaph, with bronze decorations of wreaths, coat of arms and lettering, and with bronze plates recording the names of the dead, was unveiled a year after the laying of the foundation stone, on 21st July, 1923, by Admiral Sir F. C. Doveton Sturdee, the hero of the Battle of the Falklands. The monument was subsequently dedicated by the Vicar of Swansea, and the crowd attending the ceremonies was estimated at over 20,000.

The memorial had been designed by the Borough Architect, Ernest E. Morgan. Unfortunately, down the years, the history of the cenotaph has not been without blemishes. Four cannons, relics of the Crimean War, and placed alongside the monument, were melted down in aid of the war effort in 1941, three ornamental gates were stolen in the mid-sixties, and severe weather and vandals have from time to time defaced the stonework and bronze plaques.

In 1986 ex-servicemen mounted a round-the-clock guard on the memorial after it had been daubed with slogans for the second successive year. The slogans included "Fight war, not wars," and "No Remembrance means no death."

Certainly the position of the memorial is a rather exposed and isolated one, and unsuccessful attempts have been made over the years to have the Cenotaph re-sited, perhaps to a new location in front of the Guildhall. This will perhaps be necessary in the future if erosion and vandalism continue to be problems, but at present the memorial appears well-tended and maintained.

It had been hoped to unveil the cenotaph in Clarence Place, Newport, on 8th May, 1923, the eighth anniversary of the Battle of Ypres action in which the Monmouthshire Regiment had suffered heavy casualties.

However, the contract for building the memorial at a cost of £2,996 had not been completed by that date and so the ceremony took place on the 2nd June, the unveiling being performed by the Lord Lieutenant of Monmouth, Major General the Right Honourable Lord Treowen.

The cenotaph is still an impressive monument but is today rather hemmed in by traffic lights and road signs, and with an overpowering modern office block as a background.

The illuminated Roll of Honour prepared as part of the memorial is now housed in the Newport Central Library.

The Middlesbrough memorial is in the form of a cenotaph standing in front of ornate park gates from which walls extend on either side. On the walls are metal tablets inscribed with the names of the men commemorated.

229   *The Newport Memorial*

The Halifax war memorial, a stone Cenotaph, was designed by H. Scott Davies of Manchester and built by J. White and Sons, the Birmingham stonemasons who made many war memorials.

The unveiling ceremony was on Sunday, 15th October, 1922, and was performed by Sir George Fisher-Smith, the dedication being offered by Bishop Frodsham, Vicar of Halifax and Senior Chaplain of the 49th (West Riding) Division.

The procession from the Town Hall to the memorial site was a most comprehensive one, consisting of Police Escort, Fire Brigade, St. John's Ambulance, Church Lads' Brigade, Boys' Brigade, Boy Scouts, Constabulary Band, Military, Ex-Servicemen, Clergy, Chief Constable, Mace Bearer, Mayor and Town Clerk, Sir George Fisher-Smith, Lt. Col. Whitley, Freemen of the Borough, Deputy Mayor and Mayor's Chaplain, Bishop Frodsham and Canon Foley, Magistrates, Magistrates' Clerk, Coroner, Aldermen, Councillors, Board of Guardians, Borough Officials, Halifax Insurance Committee, War Pensions Committee, Halifax Chamber of Commerce, Halifax Chamber of Trade, Halifax Commercial Travellers' Association, and finally a further Police Escort.

Today the memorial, some distance from the town centre, appears to be in some danger from vandals, with some graffiti in evidence and a considerable amount of broken glass around the site. A large imposing building behind the monument is closed, with its ground floor windows boarded.

The Cenotaph which is Hull's memorial to the Great War, when 70,000 out of a population of 290,000 answered the call for men, is situated in Paragon Square in the centre of the city.

It was unveiled on 20th September, 1924, by
Field Marshal Sir William Robertson.
Immediately in front of it is the memorial to the
dead of the South African War.

Elsewhere in Hull is another surviving
street memorial of the Great War. Behind a glass
front, and inside an ornate timber frame
decorated with likenesses of King George V and
allied generals and admirals, is the Sharp
Street Roll of Honour.

This lists the names of about 140 men from
the street who served in the war, 11 of them
giving their lives.

Sometimes memorials were designed to
incorporate both a cenotaph and sculptured
figures, either of a military or of a more general
nature. The Portsmouth memorial was an
example of this.

Another example can be found at Croydon
where the war memorial, on a prominent site by
the Town Hall, is in the form of a Cenotaph
supported by a stone shaft, at the foot of which
are two bronze figures. The first is of a wounded

233   *The Croydon Memorial*

234   *The Croydon Memorial: detail*

127

235   *The Croydon Memorial: detail*

soldier of the East Surrey Regiment, tending his own wound, and the other is of a woman holding a young child, while seeming to reach out to the injured man.

Both figures are seated and on the stonework separating them is the inscription,

A TRIBUTE TO THE MEN AND WOMEN OF CROYDON WHO DIED AND SUFFERED.

High above the inscription is a bronze cross.

The Bradford memorial was unveiled on Saturday 1st July, 1922, the sixth anniversary of the first day of the Battle of the Somme, when the Bradford 'Pals' Battalion of the West Yorkshire Regiment had suffered such heavy casualties.

The unveiling, before a crowd of 40,000, was carried out by Lieutenant-Colonel Alderman Anthony Gadie, a former Lord Mayor who had served in France with the Royal Artillery. The dedication was by the Vicar of Bradford, Archdeacon W. Stanton Jones. Field Marshal Earl Haig, a freeman of the city, was unable to attend, but another freeman, who had been elected on 13th September, 1921, to represent all ex-servicemen, ex-Sergeant J. W. Robertshaw, took part in the ceremony.

The memorial was in the form of a Cenotaph of Bolton Wood stone, supported by the bronze figures of a soldier and a sailor, while high up on the front was a stone cross symbolising Sacrifice.

The designer was the City Architect, Walter Williamson, and the site chosen was the prominent one of Victoria Square, in front of the statue of Queen Victoria.

In addition to the Cenotaph there was a Roll of Honour, with the names of nearly 37,000 Bradford men who served in the war, of whom about 5,000 were killed, and this was placed in the Central Free Library.

The memorial's two bronze figures, lunging forward with fixed bayonets, were

236   *The Bradford Memorial*

237   *The Bradford Memorial: detail*

238   *The Bradford Memorial: detail*

criticized for being too warlike and aggressive and it was felt by many that they "did not strike the right note," to quote the Lord Mayor.

In the 1960's the offending bayonets were deliberately twisted and bent, either by vandals or by peace campaigners, and when the memorial was subsequently cleaned they were not replaced. The figures are still without bayonets which, unfortunately, makes them appear unbalanced and detracts from what is a fine monument.

Sculptured military figures were as popular in large communities as elsewhere.

Another memorial featuring figures of a soldier and a sailor is that in the Diamond in Londonderry. The sculptor was Vernon March of Farnborough, whose design was selected from 115 submitted. On a centre pedestal, about 20ft. high, is a winged Victory and on two lower pedestals are the figures of the servicemen.

The soldier, in particular, would not have drawn wholehearted approval from the critics in Bradford who felt that their memorial figures were too aggressive. The Londonderry figure, with rifle raised above shoulder height, and about to strike downwards with the bayonet, was

239
The Keighley Memorial, Yorkshire

129

240   *The Keighley Memorial: detail*

241   *The Keighley Memorial: detail*

described as a "vivid and realistic piece of work. The attitude of the figure suggests with great intensity a leading feature of the war — the attack upon an entrenched enemy, and the effect is intensified by the elevation of the pedestal."

Keighley's 35ft. high memorial with its supporting bronze figures of a soldier and a sailor, and surmounted by a bronze figure of Victory, was designed by Henry C. Fehr who had earlier been responsible for the Leeds memorial, and who also worked on those at Colchester and Eastbourne.

On 7th December, 1924, over 20,000 people attended the unveiling ceremony by Lieutenant-General Sir Charles Harington, who was G.O.C. Northern Command. The memorial commemorated some 900 men of the town, and children of those who had fallen were allowed to stand at the front of the huge crowd so that they could more easily lay wreaths at the end of the ceremony.

The mayor of Poix-du-Nord, Keighley's adopted French town, attended and presented a bronze laurel wreath which remained at the base of the memorial for many years before apparently disappearing in the 1970's. The figure of the soldier has also suffered from the attention of vandals, his rifle strap and bayonet having been removed. Despite this, the memorial is a very impressive one, and the bronzes are particularly fine.

The Cambridgeshire war memorial, on a prominent site in Hills Road, Cambridge, was unveiled on 3rd July, 1922, by the Duke of York.

An 8ft. bronze figure in Cambridgeshire Regiment uniform, it is named "The Home-Coming" and the stride of the soldier is

242   *The Cambridge Memorial*

130

2ins. longer than normal to give a feeling of elation. On his back is a pack and a captured German helmet, on his left shoulder is his rifle over which is hung a laurel wreath, and in his right hand he is carrying his own helmet and a rose.

On the base of the memorial are the words,
TO THE MEN OF CAMBRIDGESHIRE THE ISLE OF ELY THE BOROUGH AND UNIVERSITY OF CAMBRIDGE WHO SERVED IN THE GREAT WAR.

The sculptor of the figure was Tait McKenzie who also sculpted the Scottish American memorial in Princes Street, Edinburgh. The figure was modelled in his studio at the University of Pennsylvania and a similar figure was commissioned for Woodbury, New Jersey. The main difference in the two is in the modelling of the heads of the young men. Apparently studies of students at Christ's College were used for the Cambridgeshire memorial while "an American type" was used for Woodbury.

It seems that the preparations for the unveiling did not proceed without difficulty. The bronze figure was not cast in time and a bronzed plaster replica was used for the ceremony with fears for its reaction to heavy rain. Apparently all went well and the actual bronze was erected ten days later.

The Twickenham memorial, in Radnor Gardens, by the banks of the Thames, was unveiled on Wednesday, 2nd November, 1921, by Field Marshal Sir William Robertson. There was a large attendance in spite of the drenching rain, and newspaper photographs show a sea of umbrellas at the scene of the unveiling.

In attendance was the Band of the Royal Military School of Music, from nearby Kneller Hall.

The monument takes the form of a bronze figure by Mortimer Brown, on a stone plinth with three bronze relief panels. The figure is of a soldier striding forward with one arm raised high, and waving his cap in greeting. The gesture, and the happy expression on the face, make a strong contrast to the more conventional attitude of mourning, with head bowed and rifle reversed, to be found in many war memorial figures.

The bronze panels show scenes representing the Navy, Air Force, and Women's Services.

Streatham's war memorial was dedicated and unveiled in the Garden of Remembrance at the corner of Streatham Common, on Saturday, 14th October, 1922. A crowd of some 5,000 attended as General Sir Charles Monro unveiled the monument which was dedicated by the Bishop of Southwark.

The garden is a pleasant one laid out on two levels, with attractive trees, lawns and flower beds, and a generous number of wooden benches. At times in its history there have been complaints that the area has been untidy and neglected, but this is not so at present.

The garden is dominated by the memorial, a bronze statue of a bare-headed soldier with rifle reversed, on a stone plinth, and with a low stone and metal surround. The bronze was sculpted by Albert T. Toft in 1921.

In addition to the garden and the statue, public subscription provided for a Roll of

243   *The Twickenham Memorial: detail*

244   *The Twickenham Memorial: detail*

245 *The Streatham Memorial*

Merton and Lady Russell-Cotes.

After their deaths, but in accordance with their wishes, on 27th July, 1926, an extension to the gallery was opened and a war memorial unveiled.

The memorial was erected in the grounds of the museum on the East Cliff and faced the sea and the pier. It was about 30ft. in height and made of Portland Stone, and consisted of three life-size figures representing the Army, Navy and Air Force and a larger female figure holding laurel wreaths in her outstretched arms above them, all on a large stone pedestal. The sculptor was Mr. George Maile and the unveiling was carried out by the Countess of Malmesbury.

Unfortunately, what photographs show to be an attractive and imposing memorial, no longer exists. It apparently weathered very badly in its exposed cliff top position until it virtually disintegrated and the site is now occupied by a "Geological Terrace."

The Sheffield war memorial, in Barker's Pool in front of the City Hall, was unveiled on Wednesday, 28th October, 1925, by Lieut.-General Sir Charles H. Harington, G.O.C. Northern Command, and dedicated by the Bishop of Sheffield.

The official party, including not only the principals and the Mayor, City Council and officers, but also representatives of the Cutlers' Company and of Sheffield University, assembled at the Town Hall and moved in procession to the Cathedral where a service was conducted by the Vicar of Sheffield, Archdeacon J. R. Derbyshire, and an address was given by the Bishop.

Honour, with the names of the 720 or so who died, to be placed in the Streatham library, and for a house adjoining the Garden of Remembrance, "The Chimes," to be used as a United Services Club. The house was eventually destroyed during the air raids of the Second World War.

The Russell-Cotes Art Gallery and Museum was presented to Bournemouth in 1916 by Sir

246　　*The Russell-Cotes Memorial, Bournemouth*

247　　*The Sheffield Memorial*

From there the procession moved on to the memorial site where the band of the Queen's Own Yorkshire Dragoons had been playing appropriate selections. During the ceremony itself buglers of the York and Lancashire Regiment sounded the *Last Post* and *Reveille*.

The memorial, by architect C. D. Carus Wilson and sculptor George Alexander, is an unusual one, being an enormously high flag-pole on a massive, and very ornate bronze base. This beautifully worked base is decorated by the figures of four soldiers with rifles reversed and heads bowed, and by coats of arms representing the army, navy, air force, city, Yorkshire Dragoons (Queen's Own), Royal Artillery, Royal Engineers, Machine Gun Corps, Tank Corps, York and Lancaster Regiment, Medical Corps, and the Royal Army Service Corps.

The principal inscription on the war memorial in front of the Royal Exchange reads,

TO THE IMMORTAL HONOUR OF THE OFFICERS,
NON-COMMISSIONED OFFICERS AND MEN OF
LONDON WHO SERVED THEIR KING AND EMPIRE IN
THE GREAT WAR 1914-1919. THIS MEMORIAL IS
DEDICATED IN PROUD AND GRATEFUL RECOGNITION
BY THE CITY AND COUNTY OF LONDON.

On the back of the memorial there is inscribed a list of London battalions, from those of the London Regiment to those of the Artillery, Yeomanry and Engineers.

The monument was unveiled on 12th November, 1920, by the Duke of York, and was designed by Sir Aston Webb, the sculptor being Alfred Drury. Two bronze military figures, one on either side of the main stone column of the memorial, are particularly impressive, and the

249   *The Royal Exchange Memorial, London*

column is surmounted by the figure of a lion supporting a shield with the figure of St. George and the dragon in relief.

Amongst the most beautiful of First World War Memorials is that of Exeter. The main bronze figure of "Victory" was in fact given pride of place in the Royal Academy Exhibition of 1922, dominating the quadrangle giving access to Burlington House, and a further bronze of a prisoner of war was also exhibited and highly praised that year. One reviewer stated, "Exeter will be happy in the possession of a war memorial of unparalleled distinction."

The completed work, in fact, has four bronze figures decorating a massive base and pedestal of Devonshire granite which is surmounted by the 8ft. tall figure of Victory standing upon a dragon, with a sword in her left hand and laurel in the right, and with her right arm extended above her head. As well as The Prisoner of War, the figures on the base are The Soldier, The Sailor, and The Nurse.

The sculptor and designer was Mr. John Angel, a native of Exeter, and the figures were cast by Mr. A. B. Burton of Thames Ditton (Victory and Prisoner of War) and by Mr. William Morris of Brixton (Soldier, Sailor and Nurse). The Exeter architects, Messrs. Greenslade & Challice, co-operated in the design of the pedestal, which was raised and worked by Easton & Son of Exeter. The whole monument is 31ft. high from the base to the laurel, and stands in a commanding position on Northernhay with the ruins of Rougemont Castle in the background.

248   *The Royal Exchange Memorial, London*

The memorial was unveiled on 24th July, 1923, by Admiral of the Fleet Earl Beatty and dedicated by the Bishop of Crediton. Earl Beatty had earlier been made a Freeman of the City, the second admiral to be so honoured, the first having been Nelson after his victory at the Nile in 1801.

A casket containing the names of the 970 of Exeter who had given their lives in the war, had been placed in a cavity within the memorial, and these names were also inscribed in a book to be kept in the city archives.

Sculptures of subjects other than servicemen were, again, widely represented. In its account of the unveiling ceremony of the Derby war memorial to some 2,000 dead, the *Derbyshire Advertiser* described the memorial itself, designed by the sculptor Arthur G. Walker, as follows:

"The Monument is a beautiful conception in bronze and stone, typifying the widowed mother, grief stricken but proud and courageous, holding her fatherless boy, with the Cross in the background."

The notes in the souvenir booklet issued at the time of the ceremony put a slightly different interpretation on the work —

"So here the whole vision is embodied in a typical English mother, bowed with her sorrow but not broken-hearted, for she is not alone in her grief, she is but one of a countless number of similar sufferers and she is thrilled with the glory of the great sacrifice of her son — cherishing the younger boy, who while clinging to his mother in perfect confidence, looks out and reaches out . . ."

The description in the booklet should perhaps be taken as the official interpretation of the memorial which was unveiled by Alderman Ling in the Market Place on Armistice Day,

252   *The Derby Memorial*

Tuesday, 11th November, 1924, and dedicated by the Bishop of Derby. Amongst the wreaths then laid at the foot of the memorial was one by the mother of the late Private Rivers, Derby's only Great War V.C.

In addition to building the monument, the city also endowed a hospital bed at the local infirmary in memory of the dead and a cheque

for £1,000 was handed over for that purpose during the ceremony.

The delightful embankment gardens are the site of the 1922 War Memorial for Bedford. The memorial, a stone figure of Justice Triumphant over Evil is the work of Charles S. Jagger, a promising young sculptor who died at an early age, and who worked also on the G.W.R. and Artillery monuments.

The memorial surround was designed by G. P. Allen, but unfortunately the chains seen linking the pillars in early photographs, no longer seem to be in existence (see Plate C27, p.113).

Newcastle's war memorial scheme commenced with the inauguration in 1920 of a "Shilling Fund" to raise the required finance for a suitable tribute. The target was 300,000 shillings and day after day, for weeks, the papers were full of lists of subscribers and news of progress towards the required figure.

The amount aimed at was achieved in a surprisingly short time and the final figure was well over £16,000.

The monument subsequently commissioned was designed by Mr. C. L. Hartwell, and its main feature is a bronze group of St. George, the Patron Saint of the Northumberland Fusiliers, mounted on a rearing horse, and in the act of killing with his lance the dragon beneath the horse's hooves. The bronze is on a high stone base, the overall height of the memorial being 32ft. of which the bronze group is about one third.

On the front of the base is the figure of a lion cut into the stone, and at each end is a bronze panel, one representing "Peace" and the other "Justice."

The memorial cost £13,260 and the balance of over £3,000 was passed to the Governors of the Royal Victoria Infirmary, Newcastle, for the provision and endowment of additional beds, with the stipulation that preferential use of the beds should be reserved for ex-servicemen who were recommended for treatment.

The monument was unveiled in Eldon Square on Wednesday, 26th September, 1923, by Field Marshal Earl Haig who, after several other official duties in the city later visited the memorial "The Response," given to the city by Sir George and Lady Renwick, and expressed his approval of its realism.

253   *The Newcastle Memorial*

254   *The Plymouth Memorial, as it was*

The memorial to the dead of Plymouth is at the entrance to the Hoe nearest to the city. Early photographs show an uninterrupted view from the city memorial to the naval one close by, but in recent years a clubhouse has surprisingly been allowed close behind the city monument, reducing its effect considerably, and cutting off the clear view through to the naval monument.

Plymouth's memorial is constructed of grey unpolished Cornish granite, a wall in a half circle enclosing a bronze female figure 8ft. 4ins. in height, holding a wreath of laurels and a sword. The architects were Messrs. Thornely & Rooke and the sculptor Mr. Birnie Rhind of Edinburgh. The Roll of Honour was sealed in a leaden casket inside the structure. The unveiling was performed by the Earl of Derby on 19th May, 1923.

256   *The Blackley Memorial, Lancashire*

The Book of Remembrance of Blackley War Memorial, Manchester, describes the monument as follows,

"It consists of a massive pedestal in best quality Stancliffe stone standing upon a platform. The pedestal is surmounted by an exquisite figure of Victory with outstretched wings, and at the foot of the pedestal, under the main inscription, is a large bronze wreath. Around the pedestal are four stone pillars, upon which are bronze figures, each bearing an emblem of one of those branches of the service which made such tremendous sacrifices in the war, viz. the Navy, the Army, the Air Force, the Nurses. The names of our fallen heroes are cast in bronze upon three name plates affixed to the sides of the pedestal.
The Memorial has been designed by Mr. L. F. Roslyn, R.B.S., the eminent London Sculptor, by whom the models for the bronze work have been executed."

The book, issued when the memorial to the 349 Blackley men who died was unveiled on Saturday, 28th May, 1921, also states,

"Blackley is proud of the indomitable spirit and heroism of the flower of her manhood, and with loving gratitude, in storied page and sculptured bronze would keep evergreen the memory of her Glorious Dead."

The printed words seem ironic today when the lower bronze figures have disappeared, the bronze wreath has been stolen, some of the inscribed name plaques have been removed, and the stone work is covered by graffiti.

If the authorities are unable to protect what remains of the memorial, admittedly in an isolated position in the park of Boggart Hole Clough, then removal to a more central site would seem to offer the only chance of its survival.

The Finsbury memorial on Spa Green, Rosebery Avenue, E.C.1., was unveiled on 15th September, 1921, by the Mayor, Alderman Lieut.-Colonel Sir Henry Barton, and dedicated by the Archdeacon of London, the Venerable E. E. Holmes.

Designed by Thomas Rudge, the memorial

257   *The Finsbury Memorial*

is a bronze figure representing Peace and Victory, on a pedestal of Cornish grey granite. Originally there were three bronze panels on the pedestal, each depicting an engagement in which Finsbury men had participated. Unfortunately, only one remains, the other two having been stolen from the memorial and not yet recovered. The remaining one commemorates the attack on Gaza, in Palestine, involving a battalion of the Finsbury Rifles, on 17th April, 1917. The two missing panels showed a naval attack at Zeebrugge on St. George's Day, 23rd April, 1918, and the crossing of the River Piave, Italy, by allied forces including a battalion of the Honourable Artillery Company.

The garden in which the memorial stands is well-tended, and the main figure of the monument is well preserved. It is even more unfortunate, therefore, that vandalism has reduced the effect of the memorial by the removal of the panels which, because of their nature, cannot be replaced.

Blackburn's war memorial is situated in a beautiful memorial garden within a park, and features a bronze group on a base of Stancliffe stone from Darley Dale, with a fountain on either side.

The group by Sir Bertram Mackennel represents "the son, returning war-worn after the conflict, received by the Motherland, supported by her, and led to peace."

The symbolism must have added even greater poignancy to the ceremony of unveiling which was carried out by Mrs. Brown, who had lost four sons in the war, and who was assisted by Mrs. Gregory, Mrs. Longworth, Mrs. Lowther and Mrs. Taylor, each of whom had lost three sons.

The Lancaster Memorial, also in a beautiful garden, is situated close to the Town Hall, and was dedicated on 3rd December, 1924.

The bronze figure of an angel stands in front of a stone wall which is higher in the centre than on the flanks. The figure stands against the higher part of the wall, while on the lower sections are set the ten bronze plaques bearing the names of the men commemorated (see Plate C28, p.113).

The City of Leeds had a fine record during the First World War. Its Roll of Honour has over 10,000 names, and not the least of its sacrifices was on the first day of the Battle of the Somme, the 1st July, 1916, when the 15th Battalion West Yorkshire Regiment (the "Leeds Pals") made an attack on the heavily fortified German position at Serre but was received with such devastating fire that all its officers were either killed or wounded. Out of a total of 900 men taking part in the attack only 17 answered the subsequent roll call.

258 The Blackburn Memorial. The bronze lions' heads have been stolen since this photograph was taken in 1987

It is all the more surprising, therefore, that appeals for subscriptions for a city war memorial met with such a poor response in the years following the war.

Early suggestions were for expensive projects like an art gallery, a museum, or a children's hospital, and early in 1920, 60,000 circulars were sent out asking for subscriptions with a view to developing an area opposite the Town Hall, in a grandiose scheme likely to cost £500,000 or so. Response was very poor, and so an amended scheme designed by Sir Reginald Blomfield, at an estimated cost of £55,000, was approved.

This also had to be shelved through lack of funds and in February 1921 a desperate appeal by the mayor for a greatly reduced sum of £20,000 for a Cenotaph and a disabled Soldiers' fund, brought in only £5,300, later to increase to £6,000.

This £6,000 was from only 210 subscribers out of a population of half a million, and three of these subscribers gave £1,000 each. One of these three, Mr. Joseph Clark, suggested that a dozen people should pay for a memorial and that the city should not pretend that the whole of the population had contributed.

Finally, a memorial costing some £5,000 was designed by a London sculptor, Mr. H. C. Fehr, who had been responsible for the city's statue of James Watt in City Square. The new memorial, also sited in City Square, was of white Carrera marble and surmounted by a bronze winged figure of "Victory" with a sword in her right hand and a wreath in her left. This figure was 11ft. in overall height, from the bronze base to the wing tips. The total height of the monument was 31ft.

On two sides of the plinth were bronze figures representing "Peace," a female figure holding a dove aloft, and "War," St. George slaying the dragon.

On Saturday, 14th October, 1922, the completed memorial was unveiled by Viscount Lascelles and dedicated by the Vicar of Leeds, the Reverend B. O. F. Heywood. The question of whether the scale of the memorial was appropriate for a city the size of Leeds was set aside and forgotten, and on the day of the ceremony a large crowd filled the square and the surrounding streets, and the monument with its white marble and fine bronzes looked an imposing and fitting tribute.

This, however, was only a temporary state of affairs. To satisfy traffic requirements the monument was moved from City Square and is now sited in a much less prominent position in the Headrow.

The figure of Victory was felt to be unsafe and was removed, therefore reducing the overall height of the memorial by a third. The remainder of the memorial was capped, to disguise the absence of the statue, which was re-erected at

260   *Leeds, the monument now*

138

261   *Leeds, the vandalized figure of Victory*

Cottingley Crematorium where it is today in a truly sorry state, with both arms broken off, and in need of cleaning and general attention. It is also sited in the middle of a rose-bed so that, when the roses are in full bloom, the lower part of the figure is hidden from view.

On 6th June, 1919, at a public meeting in Colchester Town Hall, it was decided to erect as a war memorial, a sculptured monument costing up to £3,000, and a memorial block at the Essex County Hospital.

On 1st January, 1920, after public contributions of some £7,500 had been received, a sum of £4,420 allocated to eventual hospital expenditure was invested, and £3,000 was handed to the Monument Committee.

At this time Viscount and Viscountess

Cowdray generously gifted to Colchester, as a memorial, the Castle and extensive grounds and it was at the entrance to the Castle that the monument was subsequently erected. The monument consists of a 16ft. high pedestal of Portland stone on three steps of granite. On top of the pedestal is a figure of Victory sculpted by Fehr, who completed a similar figure for the Eastbourne memorial. The winged figure holds in her right hand a sword, point down, to represent the "Cross of Sacrifice and Sword of Devotion," and in her left hand a laurel wreath.

At the base of the pedestal are two further bronzes, one of St. George standing on a dead dragon, and one of Peace.

The two lower figures are 7ft. high, the Victory figure is 11ft. high, and the total height of the monument is 28ft. 6ins. A most impressive memorial, on a prominent site with the Castle in the background, it was unveiled by General Lord Horne to the memory of 1,248 dead whose names are in a casket in the foundations of the monument, along with several other items including medals.

Eastbourne's memorial to the 1,056 men and women who fell in the Great War was unveiled on 10th November, 1920.

It is in a prominent town centre position and is surmounted by a bronze by Fehr, of a winged female figure holding aloft a laurel wreath and a sword with its point downwards, as if the weapon were a cross.

On a large bronze plate on the plinth is the inscription,

THE TRIBUTE OF EASTBOURNE TO HER GALLANT SONS AND DAUGHTERS WHO WERE FAITHFUL UNTO DEATH IN THE GREAT WAR. THEIR NAMES ARE RECORDED ON OAK TABLETS IN THE TOWN HALL.

The Preston war memorial was unveiled on Sunday, 13th June, 1926, by Admiral of the Fleet Earl Jellicoe of Scapa.

Designed by Sir Giles Gilbert Scott and with sculpture by Henry Pegram, it was erected in the city's Market Square, in front of the Post Office building, and on the spot formerly occupied by the South African War Memorial which was

262
The Colchester Memorial

263   *The Eastbourne Memorial*

264   *The Preston Memorial (Photograph — R. Boorman)*

re-sited in Avenham Park.

The memorial consists of a Portland stone pylon some 70ft. in height, at the foot of which is a projecting sarcophagus with a bronze cross and wreath, and a sculptured stone figure of Victory holding two laurel wreaths aloft.

On the base are inscribed the words,
BE EVER MINDFUL OF THE MEN OF PRESTON WHO FELL IN THE GREAT WAR.
and
THIS LAND INVIOLATE YOUR MONUMENT.

The memorial is still an impressive and attractive one, but there are early signs of weathering and the face of the Victory figure has been damaged.

At the time of the unveiling in July 1928 of the Bolton war memorial, designed by Mr. A. J. Hope, it was regretted that two groups of bronze figures, "Peace Restraining War" and Peace Seeing the Horrors of War" were not at that time ready, and might not be until Armistice Day 1929. It was not in fact until just before Armistice Day 1932 that the bronzes were finally placed in position on the memorial, after considerable complaint and correspondence in the local press. The sculptor, Mr. W. Marsden of South Kensington, had apparently been "waiting for inspiration."

The bronzes were placed on either side of the original memorial arch containing a bronze cross, which, four years earlier, had been unveiled in Victoria Square by Lord Derby, and dedicated by the Bishop of Manchester, Dr. Temple. Before the main ceremony the Bishop

had, in the Hall of Remembrance in the Town Hall, dedicated the Roll of Honour with the names of 3,510 men and women of Bolton who fell in the war.

The Accrington memorial stands high up in a parkland setting, with extensive views before it. It is built on a sloping site, and takes the form of a stone obelisk and the stone figure of a mourning woman, upon a massive and elaborate plinth. At a lower level is a wall carrying eleven slate tablets on which are engraved the names of almost 1,000

265   *The Bolton Memorial*

140

266 *The Accrington Memorial*

men from the area who died in the war.

The monument was designed by Professor C. H. Reilly and the sculptor was G. H. Tyson Smith.

The Greenock memorial is on a high site overlooking the Firth of Clyde and a War Memorial Booklet published in 1924 makes the point that "the sea that flows by Greenock's doors is the very fount of her existence and the foundation of her prosperity." This booklet lists over 1,500 men from the town who gave their lives in the war, and who are commemorated by the memorial.

The architects, Messrs. Wright and Wylie of Glasgow, and the sculptor Andrew Proudfoot, of Glasgow, incorporated many unusual features in keeping with Greenock's maritime tradition and early history.

The granite structure consists of a high base on a broad platform, surmounted by a tall obelisk. At the base of the obelisk is the prow of a Viking ship on which is the bronze winged figure of Victory holding aloft a laurel wreath. High up on the face of the obelisk is carved a Celtic cross against which is a two-handed Scottish sword, and there are many other Celtic ornaments carved on the memorial with animal forms being freely used.

Another obelisk forms the Wolverhampton memorial. The first Wolverhampton War Memorial Committee meeting was held on 11th November, 1919, the first anniversary of the end of the war. The mayor appealed for suggestions as to the type of memorial required and these suggestions included an art gallery, a public hall, a garden city of one hundred houses for widows and orphans of the fallen, a cenotaph, a new science and technical school and a reconstruction of the local hospital.

The most popular idea was the public hall, but subsequent appeals to large local firms met with a poor response and adequate financial support was not secured, and so the scheme for the hall was abandoned.

In 1921 Mr. John W. Simpson, President of the Royal Institute of British Architects, was appointed to act as adviser and assessor on an open competition for a monument design. He suggested a £5,000 budget, and the eventual estimate for the chosen scheme was £4,955. The successful architect was C. T. Armstrong and the sculptor W. C. H. King.

The memorial, an obelisk of Red Hollington stone, was decorated by four niches containing figures representing the Army, Navy and Air Force and a figure of St. George, and the site chosen was at the south west corner of St. Peter's Collegiate Church.

268 *The Wolverhampton Memorial*

267 *The Greenock Memorial*

In May 1922 the mayor appealed to the general public for subscriptions towards a figure of £20,000 for the memorial, for playing fields and for a fund for assisting deserving cases. By the time of the unveiling of the memorial by Admiral Sir Doveton Sturdee on 2nd November, 1922, only some £6,000 had been received although the fund finally exceeded £7,000, and so some monies were eventually made available to assist widows and families of the men of the city, over 1,000 in number, who had died in the service of their country.

The site chosen for the memorial is a prominent and attractive one, and the area is well-tended, but trees which have subsequently been planted around the obelisk, although in themselves a pleasant feature, nevertheless hide the column to a very considerable extent and may eventually mask it almost completely.

Blackpool's war memorial, on the Princess Parade at the end of the Promenade, takes the form of a massive 100ft. high obelisk of Cornish granite. At its base are bronze panels of sculpture depicting "1914 — The Outbreak of War" and "1918 — The End of the War," and, to the north and south are two war stones on top of which are bronze plates with the names of the fallen. The 12ft. long war stones are replicas of those placed in war cemeteries in France.

The designer of the memorial was Ernest Prestwich of Leigh and the sculptor was Gilbert Ledward of London.

A crowd of some 30,000 people attended the unveiling ceremony on 10th November, 1923, when Brigadier-General T. E. Topping, a local man, unveiled the main monument and the war stones were unveiled by Mrs. Boughey and Mrs. Smith, the mothers of two V.C.s who were amongst the dead, 2nd Lieutenant Stanley H. P. Boughey, and Lieutenant A. Victor Smith, whose father was Chief Constable of Burnley. Each mother wore her son's decorations, including the V.C.

The memorial at Southport is a central obelisk between two colonnades.

The colonnades are built at some distance from the central feature, which is in the middle of a square, round which quite heavy traffic circulates. By contrast, the colonnades are each at the end of a pleasant garden with lawns, flower beds and fountains.

The designers of the memorial were Messrs. Gayson & Barnish, with sculpture by G. H. Tyson Smith.

The war memorial colonnade on the Old Steine, to the men and women of Brighton who

271
The Brighton Memorial

served in the Great War, was unveiled on Saturday, 7th October, 1922, by Admiral of the Fleet Earl Beatty, who also received the Freedom of the Borough that day.

The day's programme began with the granting of the Freedom to Earl Beatty at 12.30 p.m. in the Council Chamber of the Town Hall, followed by lunch at 1.30 p.m. in the Dome, Royal Pavilion.

The cost of the luncheon, to those who were required to pay, was 8s. 6d. each, "exclusive of wine, minerals and cigars," and remittance was required with the application.

The unveiling ceremony was at 3 p.m. and the subsequent dedication was by the Vicar of Brighton, the Rev. Canon Dormer Pierce. Enclosures were arranged for relatives of the dead, for subscribers, and for ex-servicemen.

During the gale which hit the south of England in October 1987, the centre of Brighton, and the vicinity of the memorial, lost a large number of trees. Damage very close to the

colonnade was extensive and there were fallen trees and debris all around it, but fortunately the structure itself was untouched.

Approximately £54,000 was subscribed for the Huddersfield war memorial of which £40,000 was invested for the benefit of the Royal Infirmary "as a tribute to the patriotism of the living who served their country," and £14,000 was spent on a "permanent monument to the illustrious dead."

The monument was designed by Sir Charles Nicholson and took the form of a Column of Victory 60ft. high, surmounted by a Sacrificial Cross, and in front of a semi-circular colonnade. This was erected on an elevated site in Greenhead Park, Huddersfield, at the top of a long and impressive flight of steps.

The completed memorial was unveiled on Saturday, 26th April, 1924 by Lieutenant-General Sir Charles Harington, G.O.C. Northern Command, and dedicated by the Vicar of Huddersfield, Canon Tupper-Carey. The

272
The Huddersfield Memorial

Huddersfield Choral Society sang the Hallelujah Chorus and the National Anthem.

The monument is, today, still a most imposing one, but, although Greenhead Park is generally very attractive and well maintained, the area of the memorial is slightly remote and rather less tidy. The stonework has some graffiti on it although the lower half of the front of the colonnade and the lower half of the column appear to have been treated to counteract this form of vandalism.

Comparatively few crosses were erected as memorials in the larger towns. The War Memorial Committee at Oxford was first formed on 28th May, 1919. After a public meeting it was decided that the memorial should take the form of a cross, and a poll resulted in the chosen site being immediately to the south of St. Giles Church.

Nine designs were submitted and that of J. E. Thorpe of Oxford, was selected. The design was a 37ft. 6ins. high medieval cross, of 15th century Gothic style, on an octagonal pedestal.

The sides of the pedestal were decorated by the dedication shield, flanked by shields bearing the arms of the City and the University, and five further shields carved with the following emblems: the Anchor (Navy), the Bugle (Land

275
The Clark Family

Forces), Wings (Air Forces), the Red Cross (Royal Army Medical Corps) and the St. George's Cross.

Clipsham stone was used for the construction and a tender for £1,200, from Oxford builders Wooldridge & Simpson, was accepted.

The cross was unveiled on Saturday, 9th July, 1921, by Major-General Sir Robert Fanshawe and dedicated by the Lord Bishop of Oxford, Dr. H. M. Burge.

The expenses of the memorial amounted to £1,500, all of which was subscribed by the time of the unveiling, partly due to the generosity of Messrs. Hall's Oxford Brewery Limited, who after giving one subscription, also gave the whole sum still outstanding, shortly before the day of the ceremony.

The 1927 war memorial at the entrance to Victoria Park, Bath, is in the form of a "Cross of Sacrifice" as designed by Sir Reginald Blomfield for the British War Cemeteries overseas.

It is backed by a curved wall on which are fixed bronze tablets with the names of the dead. The mayor of Bath, Alderman Cedric Chivers, personally provided the tablets while the estimated cost of the memorial itself, some £3,000, was sought from general subscription after the scheme had been approved at a "Citizens Meeting" held in the Guildhall on 21st September, 1925.

Amongst the names on the bronze tablets are those of three Clark brothers, Bertie who died in Belgium aged 20, Sidney who died in France in 1916 aged 20, and Edward who died in France in 1916 aged 32.

The Bath Herald, like many local papers, published a "Roll of Honour" at frequent intervals to give information about casualties and a photograph of Private Sidney Clark, of the London Regiment, appeared on Saturday, 4th November, 1916, while that of Private E. L. Clark, Canadian Contingent, appeared on Saturday, July 29th, 1916.

276   *The Chelsea Memorial*

A family photograph taken in about 1907 in the garden of the Gayshill Tavern, Bath, where the father of the family, Frank Clark, was publican, shows the three boys who eventually died in the war, a decade or so later.

In this photograph of the parents and their twelve children, Bertie is believed to be the boy sitting next to his mother, Sidney is in the front, and Edward is third from the left in the back row.

After unsuccessful negotiations with the Commissioners of the Royal Hospital about a site for a Chelsea War Memorial, the local council in 1919 adopted the idea of erecting the memorial in Sloane Square. Two appeals to the public followed, just as was necessary in so many towns and villages throughout the country at that time. The first was an appeal for the money required to build the monument, and the second was for information about the men who had died in the war and whose names were to be

commemorated.

The first appeal published was worded as follows,

"ALL CHELSEA PEOPLE are invited to join and help in the erection of a
WAR MEMORIAL CROSS
to the Memory of Chelsea Men who gave their lives for their country in the Great War.

This "Cross of Sacrifice," of which a photograph is reproduced on the other side, is to the design by
Sir Reginald Blomfield, R.A.,
which has been adopted by the Government for the Cemeteries of Our Dead in France and elsewhere. It will be about 24ft. high, and is to be placed, with the sanction of the Borough Council, on the Western Island in Sloane Square.

Subscriptions (and small or large sums are equally welcome) will be received and acknowledged on behalf of the Committee by
Miss L. W. Kempson
S.W. London Polytechnic, Manresa Road, Chelsea, S.W.3."

The second appeal, for information, read,
"Metropolitan Borough of Chelsea
ROLL OF HONOUR
The War Memorial Committee of the Chelsea Borough Council are desirous of compiling, in connection with the Local Official War Memorial, a complete list of all Chelsea residents (both men and women) who were killed, or have died from wounds, or other causes, whilst on active service, and would, therefore, be glad if persons possessing information relating to such residents would kindly furnish me with the necessary particulars. Forms containing details of the information required may be obtained from my office.
T. HOLLAND, TOWN CLERK.
Town Hall, King's Road, Chelsea, S.W.3."

The cross was eventually erected on the proposed site and on the 24th October, 1920, was unveiled by Field Marshal Sir William Robertson and dedicated by the Archdeacon of Middlesex.

The War Memorial Committee of the Royal Borough of Kensington managed to combine both the ornamental and the utilitarian aspects of possible war memorials, discussions about these two usually mutually exclusive aspects taking up many hours of committee time throughout the country after the war.

The Kensington memorial consisted of a monument built at the junction of Kensington High Street and Church Street, on land which was previously part of the churchyard of St. Mary Abbots, and also the Kensington Memorial Park, a playing field and park on land purchased from a Mr. W. St. Quintin by the Borough Council, and opened on 24th June, 1926.

The monument, designed by Major H. C. Corlette, is inscribed with the principal battle honours of the two Kensington regiments which served in the war, the 22nd Kensington Service Battalion, the Royal Fusiliers City of London Regiment; and the 13th Princess Louise's Kensington Battalion, the London Regiment.

277   *The Kensington Memorial*

146

Above the base on which the inscriptions are carved, is a stone with the arms of the Royal Borough in heraldic colours and on this stone stands the sculptured figure of a woman by F. W. Pomeroy. In her left hand is a laurel wreath and in her right is a scroll which she lifts up to place against the memorial, the scroll bearing the words from *Henry V*, "Awake remembrance of the valiant dead."

Above this piece of sculpture the main pillar of the memorial rises to the figures of four winged angels, above which is the Cross.

The war memorial committee had been assisted in their choice of design by Alderman Sir Aston Webb, President of the Royal Academy.

The unveiling ceremony was on Saturday, 1st July, 1922, when the unveiling was performed by Princess Louise, Duchess of Argyll, and the dedication by the Bishop of Kensington.

The unveiling of the Lincoln war memorial on Wednesday, 25th October, 1922, was preceded by a service in the Cathedral and by an impressive procession through crowds lining the mile-long route from the Cathedral to St. Benedict's Square.

There are no longer railings and gates around the memorial site, but on the day of the ceremony the key to the gates was first handed to Field Marshal Sir William Robertson, and, after the formal opening of the gates and a well-received speech, he unveiled the memorial which was subsequently dedicated by the Bishop of Lincoln.

During his speech Sir William mentioned the fact that the men of Lincolnshire had raised eleven battalions of the county regiment as well as contributing to many other services. The 1st Battalion "captured the first battery of artillery ever obtained in the war" and the French authorities in the vicinity of the Hohenzollern Redoubt "where the 4th Regiment fought so well and lost so many," had sent over a wreath of the flowers growing on the graves of the men there.

The minutes of a meeting, held on 13th November, 1920, of the Executive Committee for the Worcestershire County War Memorial, gives a great deal of information about the choice and financing of this project.

At the time the position of the Fund was as follows:

Paid to Bank	£9,156	12.	10.
Bank Interest	£173	1.	10.
Subscriptions promised	£444	0.	0.
	£9,773	14.	8.
Various expenses. Printing, etc.	£193	0.	6.
Transferred to Relief Fund	£5,000	0.	0.
	£5,193	0.	6.
Balance available for Memorials	£4,580	14.	2.

An earlier public advertisement issued by the committee had invited designs for a permanent monument. The cost was not to exceed £2,000 and it was stipulated that the monument should not take the form of statuary.

Sixteen designs were received and five were selected for submission to the Dean and Chapter, to seek approval for the erection of any one of them in the Cathedral precincts. It was suggested by the Dean that the site for the memorial should be as near as possible to that of the existing, presumably temporary, Cenotaph, as that site had become associated in the minds of many with those who fell in the war.

Eventually the choice was a design similar to that of a cross erected in Herefordshire, photographs of this being made available to the committee. In addition to the outside monument a design for a stained glass window to be placed in the Cathedral as part of the county memorial was prepared by Mr. J. Eadie Reid, and it was also proposed to place commemorative tablets and books in the Cathedral.

The administration of the Relief Fund, to which £5,000 had been transferred, was discussed, and it was reported that since the formation of the fund in May 1919, 128 applications for assistance had been received and 89 cases had been helped. Of these 22 were widows and dependants and 67 were disabled ex-servicemen. Grants of £1,174 had been made together with loans of £364 of which £133 had been repaid. The loans had been chiefly to start disabled men in occupation.

The minutes of later meetings discussed the proposed unveiling of the Memorial Window on Armistice Day 1921, and the Memorial Cross a year later on Armistice Day 1922.

278   *The Lincoln Memorial*

279   *The Worcester Memorial*

Minutes of later meetings of the Relief sub-committee show entries such as a grant of £25 to H. Newick to buy a dray on 22nd March, 1921; a grant of £6 to H. Rounds to purchase a plough on 1st February, 1921; a grant of £3 to C. Richards for clothes on 18th January, 1921; a grant of £25 to the scheme for boarding out orphan children on 1st February, 1921; a grant of £2 to buy clothes for Gladys May Biddulph, the daughter of a deceased soldier, boarded out with an aunt, on 18th January, 1924; and a grant of £5 to enable Jessie Darby to be suitably fitted out for domestic service on 18th January, 1924.

The Relief Fund was effectively wound up in 1936 after a year in which only £12. 10s. had been disbursed, and the demands upon the fund had virtually ceased. The other memorials remain, the stone cross being on a prominent roadside site close to the cathedral. On a base of eight stone steps, the cross has an octagonal plinth on the panels of which are carved badges of the Worcestershire Regiment, the Yeomanry, the Royal Field Artillery, the Royal Navy, the Royal Engineers, the R.A.S.C., the R.A.F., and the arms of the County.

Amongst memorials of other types, there was a memorial shelter at Elland Road, Churwell, Leeds, which in the last few years was vandalised to such an extent that demolition was the only possible option on the grounds of safety.

The shelter was at one end of a Garden of Remembrance, and, having realised that such shelters are frequently targets of vandals, the Leeds City Council have not attempted to replace it, but have spent money on making good the site of the building and on generally tidying up the whole garden, repainting the gates and railings, and providing sturdy outdoor benches.

Over the last two years the Municipal Services Department of Leeds has compiled a list of war memorials in the area as a first step towards their protection and, where necessary, their restoration.

The Bournemouth War Memorial Committee decided "that the memorial should be placed in a comparatively central, but not too public, a position" and certainly the chosen site in the Upper Pleasure Gardens close to the Town Hall, seems to answer that requirement.

Today the memorial is surrounded by lawns and flower beds and is attractive and well maintained. During the Second World War a bomb fell some 30 yards from it and although it was covered with mud and soil no damage was done.

The monument was designed by the deputy borough architect, E. A. Shervey, and constructed by W. A. Hoare of Boscombe. It is built of Portland stone and enclosed by a balustrade with the approach, up a short flight of steps, guarded by two lions. At each of the four corners of the memorial is a Doric column surmounted by a classical urn, and the general design was well received at the time of the unveiling on Wednesday, 8th November, 1922, by the Lord Lieutenant of Hampshire, Major-General J. E. B. Seely.

280   *The Bournemouth Memorial*

148

281
The Ealing Memorial

A Book of Remembrance with the names of 650 dead was placed in the shrine in a Hall of Memory in the Town Hall, and copies of the book were distributed to relatives.

During an appeal in 1919 about £8,000 was raised for an Ealing War Memorial. Of this sum a house-to-house collection realized £2,250 and the proceeds of an August Bank Holiday Fete were £1,946.

Of the money raised £1,574 was spent on a Memorial Gateway on Ealing Green, and the balance of over £6,000 became the "Fund of the Grateful Hearts," primarily for the purpose of making educational grants to the children of men who had died, but also to make maintenance, convalescent and general payments in cases of need.

The Memorial Gates, designed by Mr. L. Shuffrey, were erected on the Green in front of the then Public Library, and unveiled on Sunday, 13th November, 1921.

The wrought-iron gates themselves were the gift of the Corporation, in special memory of its own employees who had died, and in the pediment of the gates were placed the borough arms. Two quadrant walls carried the names of over 1,000 of the fallen and four piers, two flanking the gates and two at the extremities of the walls, were surmounted by 18th century stone vases from an old mansion which formerly stood at the south west corner of Ealing Common.

An inscription to the memory of the dead referred to them as

BEAUTIFUL EVERMORE, AND WITH THE RAYS OF MORN ON THEIR WHITE SHIELDS OF EXPECTATION.

Of the 1,000 and more names on the memorial are those of three brothers, Gordon, Victor and Dudley Millington. A family photograph taken at their home in Old Oak Road, Acton, just before the war, shows eight sons of whom five served in the forces. Arthur Gordon (aged 30) and Dudley Graham (aged 19)

282
The Millington Family

were killed on the same day, 9th May, 1915, in action with the 13th County of London Regiment. Victor was killed in an explosion later in the war whilst serving with the Ordnance Corps, while Stanley and Leslie, both in the London Rifle Brigade survived, although the latter was injured early in 1915.

In the photograph Gordon is second from the left, Victor third from the right, and Dudley on the far right of the back row.

It has already been mentioned that in cities it was not always easy for decisions to be made quickly, and for memorial schemes to be completed in a reasonable time.

At a public meeting held in Dundee as early as January 1919 it was unanimously decided to erect a war memorial to commemorate over four thousand fallen of the 30,000 Dundee men who served in the war.

Difficulties over fund-raising and indecision about the site and type of memorial required, however, led to considerable delay, and it was not until September 1923 that the War Memorial Committee, with some £12,000 in hand, accepted a tender from R. Pert & Son, Montrose, to construct a monument to the design of the architect Thomas Braddock.

Braddock's design had been selected after a competition held under the auspices of the R.I.B.A., and Sir Robert Lorimer of Edinburgh had been the assessor. Described as "an arresting monolith" the winning design was to be built of

granite with a bronze brazier surmounting it, and the site chosen was the Law, a 570ft. hill which forms a backdrop to the City. The choice of site was by no means universally approved and amongst the criticism it was suggested that the memorial would be too inaccessible and that it would destroy the hill's natural appearance.

It had been hoped to use Aberdeen granite for the construction but the tender accepted was for Cornish granite at a price of £7,950, the same contractor's figure for Aberdeen granite being £9,900.

In addition to the monument, separate permanent records of the names of the dead were prepared, one list being shown on panels on an oak stand in the Permanent Gallery of the Albert Institute and another in the form of a book placed in the Town House.

It was hoped to have the memorial unveiled in November, 1924 by Earl Haig, but a builders' strike led to considerable delay in the bronze work for the brazier and the door of the monument, the work being the responsibility of a Cheltenham firm.

Eventually, General Sir Ian Hamilton unveiled the completed monument on Saturday, 16th May, 1925. Because of the restricted nature of the site, accommodation on the Law was provided only for the platform party, aged relatives of the fallen, limbless soldiers, representatives of the various regiments, and

283   *The Dundee Memorial*

members of the Town Council and War Memorial Committee, but loudspeakers were erected so that the crowds further down the hill could follow the service and speeches.

A guard of honour was provided by the 4th/5th Black Watch and, as the monument was unveiled, pipers played *Lochaber No More*.

Sir Ian Hamilton's speech was rather more direct than many such speeches were at the time. He was forthright about the widespread unemployment of former soldiers and urged the government to start work of national importance immediately to reduce such unemployment. He also had no kind word for scientists. His speech included the following words,

> "The luminous mass of Cornish granite breaks from the Imperial colours in which it was swathed and stands four-square upon the Law where there is no reason it should not endure till the scientists who invented poison gas carry out their principles to a logical conclusion and explode their own planet."

At the conclusion of the ceremony, Sir Ian's programme included visits to "Dunalistair," the memorial holiday home established by the Black Watch at Broughty Ferry, and to houses at Barnhill erected by the Veterans' Garden City Association for the housing of disabled men.

An interesting newspaper item before the unveiling ceremony describes proceedings at a meeting of the Dundee Magistrates, when a letter was submitted from the Secretary of the Shop Assistants' Union asking the Magistrates to recommend the closing of shops for three or four hours on the afternoon of Saturday, 16th May.

Baillie Smith is reported as saying

"Ridiculous nonsense; that's the only day we get any money." Baillie Gillies thought that the Magistrates could make the recommendation and let the shopkeepers do what they wished. In the event it seems that Smith misjudged the mood of the city as on the day of the ceremony a majority of shops were closed.

Today, the memorial can be seen not only from most parts of the city but also from the surrounding countryside. To the inscription of the First World War has been added a similar one for the Second, and the memorial is well-preserved and impressive, with views from the Law over the whole city and the Tay estuary.

The Leicester war memorial was not unveiled until 4th July, 1925, and at the time of the ceremony only £16,000 had been raised towards the target of £25,000. The editorial comment in the *Leicester Advertiser* at that time was frank in its criticism.

> "It is indeed a disgrace, that nearly seven years after the cessation of hostilities we should be touting around to get money to pay for what should have been bought and paid for at least five year ago. It could have been obtained then quite easily, but dilatoriness on the part of those who had control and a lack of tact in dealing with the public, caused the whole thing to fall flat. I attended all the public meetings called (none too early) to decide upon a suitable memorial, and the impression I got, in common with others, was of an attempt to keep the decision entirely in a few hands. The public does not like that sort of thing, and it has shown its disapproval by not throwing itself into the scheme with enthusiasm. The

284   *The Leicester Memorial*

result is that Leicester, though some eight times as big as Loughborough, has had a struggle to raise as much money as Loughborough has already spent."

However, the article went on to praise the scheme which had been accepted and to express determination that the balance of the money required would be found.

The memorial, an Arch of Remembrance designed by Sir Edwin Lutyens, was erected in Victoria Park to the memory of those of the City and County who died. Made of Portland stone, it enshrines flags within the arch and on the front facing the avenue from London Road are the words:

REMEMBER IN GRATITUDE TWELVE THOUSAND MEN OF THIS CITY AND COUNTY WHO FOUGHT AND DIED FOR FREEDOM. REMEMBER ALL WHO SERVED AND STROVE AND THOSE WHO PATIENTLY ENDURED.

The unveiling was performed by Mrs. Elizabeth Ann Butler a widow, aged 69, assisted by Mrs. Annie Elizabeth Glover, also a widow, aged 53. Mrs. Butler had lost four sons in the war and had two others wounded. At the outbreak of the war she had no fewer than eleven sons and six daughters living, and eight of the sons served in the army.

Mrs. Glover was the mother of eight sons and five daughters and three of her sons were killed in action, as well as two nephews and two brothers-in-law.

The Bishop of Peterborough dedicated the memorial and a crowd of some 30,000 attended the service and the unveiling.

The scheme adopted for the Nottingham War Memorial was made possible initially by the generosity of Sir Jesse Boot, the retail chemist, in presenting 36 acres of land to the Corporation. This land had a frontage to the River Trent of over three quarters of a mile, and a considerable portion was allocated as sports grounds, while the area near the proposed war memorial site was made into ornamental and rock gardens.

The Portland stone memorial facing the river on the Victoria Embankment is a Memorial Arch flanked by curved wing walls, the total width from one wing to the other being 250ft. The three-span central archway is 46ft. in height, and ornamental wrought-iron gates fill the openings.

The coat of arms of the City appears in metal above the central gate, and also carved in stone high up on the arch. Through the archway is a terrace which looks out over the ornamental gardens.

The scheme was carried out to the design of the City Engineer, Mr. T. Wallis Gordon, and the memorial was unveiled by the Mayor, Alderman Edmund Huntsman, on Armistice Day, Friday, 11th November, 1927. The date is surprising as the foundation stone of the arch had been laid by the Prince of Wales on 1st August, 1923, but the delay was largely attributed to the enormous amount of site levelling and preparation which was necessary in the area of the memorial, work which was allotted to unemployed men and for which funds were received from the Unemployment Grants Committee.

The Coventry war memorial unveiling ceremony was not held until Saturday, 8th October, 1927, but the fact that nine years had

285   *The Nottingham Memorial*

286
*The Coventry
Memorial*

passed since the end of the war did not signify lack of interest in the scheme. In fact, the first appeal for subscriptions was in 1919 when the sum of £31,562 was raised to buy 122 acres of land for a War Memorial Park and 61 acres of Stivichall Common. The land was formally handed over to the Corporation on October 26th, 1920, and the park was dedicated and officially declared open on July 9th, 1921.

Rock gardens and other ornamental gardens were subsequently laid out, together with football and hockey pitches, tennis courts and bowling greens. The stone for the entrance gates was formerly part of the ancient city wall of Coventry.

An unusual feature was the planting, amongst other trees, of 181 copper beeches to the memory of individual men. These trees, and stones marked with the men's names, were paid for by friends or relatives, one Coventrian remembering the sum of 25/- being paid for the tree commemorating his brother, Private C. Walker.

From the first, it was the intention to erect a monument in the Park, and after a competition amongst Coventry architects the design by Mr. T. F. Tickner was selected. Although he died shortly afterwards his design of a tall graded column of stone was retained and eventually built by J. G. Gray, a Coventry contractor, under the supervision of another Coventry architect.

A further part of the scheme was a Roll of Honour to be placed in a Chamber of Silence within the monument. A further appeal in September 1924 for £5,000 to pay for the work, actually raised £5,350.

The monument, to the 2,587 Coventry war dead, was finally unveiled in 1927 by Field-Marshal Earl Haig and dedicated by the Bishop of Coventry. A crowd estimated at 60,000 attended, with a parade of ex-servicemen numbering over 4,000. The service was relayed by amplifiers to the huge assembly.

After the dedication Earl Haig unlocked the door of the Chamber of Silence and placed the Roll of Honour inside it, in a carved oak cabinet. Corporal Arthur Hutt, V.C., and Mrs. E. Bench, who had lost four sons in the war, each then placed a wreath of poppies in front of the cabinet. As the local newspaper reported, "It was a happy thought which inspired this little act in the ceremony."

Amongst other wreaths subsequently laid at the memorial was one by Earl Haig as President of the British Legion.

The War Memorial Park today, with its stately white monument, and its beautiful trees and flower beds, is a most peaceful and attractive tribute to the men who died.

The dedication of Liverpool's War Memorial did not take place until Armistice Day 1930, twelve years to the day after the end of the war. By then, as the local British Legion pointed out, Liverpool was practically the only place in the country without a permanent memorial, a temporary wooden Cenotaph having been used for many years for Remembrance ceremonies.

Several years of delay had been caused by the Lord Mayor's announcement in November 1920 that he was postponing his appeal in connection with a memorial, "in view of the amount of unemployment now existing." It was not until November 1925 that another scheme was initiated, and the following year an open competition to choose a design for the city's memorial attracted entries of 767 drawings and 39 models.

From these the design of Lionel B. Budden, Associate Professor in Architecture at Liverpool University, was chosen.

The design was for a long rectangular monument of Darley Dale stone, altar-like in shape. The site for the memorial was to be the

287   *The Liverpool Memorial (Photograph by kind permission of Liverpool Daily Post and Echo Ltd.)*

plateau below St. George's Hall, and this determined the shape and material of the design. On the stone were two long bronze friezes with figures in low relief. On the outer face, above a frieze showing figures in mourning, was the inscription,

TO THE MEN OF LIVERPOOL WHO FELL IN THE GREAT WAR,

and below it the words,

AND THE VICTORY THAT DAY WAS TURNED INTO MOURNING UNTO ALL THE PEOPLE.

The size of the original design was 39ft. long but this was later slightly reduced, and the cost was estimated at £8,000 compared with the stipulated maximum of £10,000. The sculpture was the responsibility of G. H. Tyson Smith, the well-known Liverpool sculptor.

Even after the design had been chosen there was criticism of the scheme. The choice of the site in front of St. George's Hall was felt to reduce the effect of the Hall's architecture, the removal of Disraeli's statue to the steps of the Hall to accommodate the memorial was criticized, and the scale of the memorial was questioned. However, it was pointed out that much of the criticism came from architects who had been unsuccessful in the design competition and gradually the scheme came to be more accepted.

More controversy arose when a decision was made that there should be no religious aspect to the unveiling ceremony, to avoid any division of feeling between the religious communities. Widespread condemnation of this incredible

decision resulted in a last minute change, and in the event a dedicatory prayer was offered by the chaplain of the 55th Division, the Reverend J. R. Beresford, and when a wreath was laid by the Catholic Archbishop of Liverpool, Dr. Downey, the *De Profundis* was recited. Prayers were also offered by representatives of the Free Church, the Greek Orthodox Church and the Jewish community.

Lord Derby, the Lord Lieutenant of the County, unveiled the memorial which was covered by a vast green cloth to which 12,000 poppies had been sewn by hand, and which also bore a huge Union Jack, and, in scarlet the word "Triumph." For the unveiling an electrical device had been installed requiring only the pressing of a button.

The buglers of the 2nd Battalion King's Regiment sounded the *Last Post* and the Liverpool Scottish pipers played the lament *The Flowers of the Forest*.

The Bristol war memorial to the men of the city, over 4,000 of them, who fell in the First World War, was not unveiled until 1932. The local newspaper in 1930, when even the site of a possible memorial was still under discussion, quoted an "old sailor" as saying, "Bristol responded very well to the war, but very badly to the War Memorial."

At this time the suggested site was at the northern end of Colston Avenue. An earlier suggestion, St. Augustine's Churchyard, had

154

288　　*The Bristol Memorial*

attracted little but adverse criticism and so had been dropped.

Many people felt that College Green was the proper place for the memorial and in October 1930, a petition signed by 3,587 citizens, over half of whom were ex-servicemen, was presented to the Dean and Chapter of Bristol Cathedral, setting out the case for this site. The reply in December said, "The Dean and Chapter do not find themselves able to grant the request," not least because "from many quarters we have evidence that there is a marked division of opinion among those actively interested in the scheme." The letter was signed by H. L. C. de Candole, Dean of Bristol.

This seemed to end the debate and the Colston Avenue site eventually became the scene of the unveiling by Field Marshal Sir William Birdwood on 26th June, 1932, of the cenotaph which is Bristol's war memorial. The dedication was by the Bishop of Bristol and amongst those present were the Duke and Duchess of Beaufort.

Fourteen years after the end of the war the then Mayor of Gloucester, W. L. Edwards, made an appeal to the people of the city to support a final effort to carry out a memorial scheme. As he put it, "If this appeal fails it is improbable that another attempt to erect such a Memorial will ever again be made by a Mayor of Gloucester."

289　　*The Gloucester Memorial*

His appeal was successful, and the already existing 5th Gloucester Memorial in the Park was incorporated in a scheme including as its main feature a curved Wall of Remembrance of Portland stone on which the names of some 1,300 who died were recorded on bronze tablets.

Immediately to the rear a Garden of Remembrance was built.

The plan was drawn up by Colonel N. H. Waller, the Cathedral architect, and the memorial was unveiled by the Duke of Beaufort on Saturday, 21st October, 1933, almost exactly 15 years after the war ended.

One result of the delay was that a task which was often, in any case, extremely difficult, was made almost impossible — the accurate listing of the names to be included on the memorial. On 20th May, 1933 *The Gloucester Journal & Chronicle* published a list of names which were about to be engraved, along with this request,

"The list has been made as complete as possible from official records, and it is hoped to group the names under the titles of the units of H.M. Forces in which the men served. The list is provisional and subject to correction and the supply of any names inadvertently omitted. Will any relatives or friends of men who belonged to the city, who fell in the war, and whose names are not on the list, notify the secretary of the memorial committee, 10 Clarence Street, giving full names and addresses and units of H.M. Forces in which the men served. All such additions and corrections must be sent in forthwith."

It is significant that the Mayor's earlier appeal letter had mentioned a figure of "about 1,200" dead, 100 less than were eventually listed.

Chapter VIII

National Memorials

As well as the national memorial of the Cenotaph, in London's Whitehall, which since 1920 has been the focus of the commemoration services on Remembrance Day, there are national memorials of Wales, Northern Ireland and Scotland.

There are also a number of other memorials which can be considered only national in character, although they may sometimes be comparatively limited in their scope.

The Cenotaph in Whitehall commemorates the British dead of both World Wars. Designed by Sir Edwin Lutyens, it was originally made in plaster and wood for the Victory Parade on 19th July, 1919 and it was only afterwards, in response to public demand, that it was reconstructed in its present form of Portland stone. Part of the original wooden structure was preserved at the Imperial War Museum until destroyed by a Second World War bomb.

The Times described the Cenotaph as "simple, masssive, unadorned" and its art critic spoke of "the common sense of the design" and said "Sir Edwin Lutyens has not tried to pile up a collection of architectural features."

The monument was unveiled on Armistice Day, 11th November, 1920, by King George V, who was accompanied by the Prince of Wales, the Duke of York, Prince Henry and the Duke of Connaught, all in uniform. On the stroke of 11 o'clock the King pressed a button to release the flag covering the Cenotaph, then followed the Silence which was finally broken by the Last Post. After the ceremony, the procession moved to Westminster Abbey for the funeral of the Unknown Warrior (see Plate C32, p.114).

The five 13th century lights known as the Five Sisters Window, in York Minster, were restored at the end of the war as a national monument to the 1,400 women of the Empire who gave their lives.

The cost of the work was met by some 32,000 women subscribers of whom one was Princess Mary, the King's daughter.

The window, re-leaded and cleaned and re-fixed throughout, was unveiled at 3 p.m. on Wednesday, 24th June, 1925, by the Duchess of York, later to be Queen Elizabeth. Similar

memorial services to that in the Minster were held on the same day in Canada, Australia, New Zealand, South Africa and Tasmania.

Under the window an inscription reads, SACRED TO THE MEMORY OF THE WOMEN OF THE EMPIRE WHO GAVE THEIR LIVES IN THE EUROPEAN WAR OF 1914-1918.

An adjacent oak screen alongside St. Nicholas' Chapel was dedicated at the same time by the Archbishop of York. An inscription on the panels explains that the screen records the names of the women who died, and these names are actually inside doors in the panelling. Behind each door is the list for a particular category such

290   *The Cenotaph, Whitehall*

as Queen Alexandra's Nursing Services, Queen Mary's Army Auxiliary Corps, Women's Royal Air Force, Red Cross, Canada, Australia, New Zealand, South Africa or Munition Workers, the last section having a considerable number of names.

Later that same afternoon the Duke of York, in the uniform of the East Yorkshire Regiment, of which he was Colonel-in-Chief, unveiled York's own war memorial dedicated to over 1,000 of its citizens who fell in the war.

Over 250,000 Belgian refugees had fled to Britain in 1914 at the same time as the British Expeditionary Force was crossing to Belgium to attempt to defend it against the German invasion.

On Victoria Embankment in London, opposite Cleopatra's Needle, is the Monument of Belgium's Gratitude, the architectural setting for which was designed by Sir Reginald Blomfield in 1920, with sculpture by Victor Rousseau.

In the centre of the memorial is a bronze group, far from traditional in design, on a stone base bearing the inscription —

TO THE BRITISH NATION FROM THE GRATEFUL PEOPLE OF BELGIUM 1914-1918.

Behind this centre piece and separating it from the Embankment Gardens is a curved wall with stone figures representing 'Justice' and 'Honour' to the left and right respectively.

The stone of the memorial is unfortunately, beginning to show signs of weathering, even the principal inscription now being less clear than it should be.

At the beginning of the Great War the Royal

Pavilion, and other buildings in Brighton, were allocated for use as a hospital for Indian casualties and sick. The bodies of those Hindus and Sikhs who died were cremated after customary religious rites at a burning ghat high up on the Downs near Patcham, about four miles north-east of Brighton. The bodies of Mohammedans were taken to their own cemetery in Woking where they were buried, also with appropriate rites.

Subsequently at Patcham, on the site of the ghat, a monument was built in the form of a "Chattri," a dome supported on pillars and purely Indian in architecture. The design was, in fact, by E. C. Henriques of Bombay.

The marble dome is 8ft. in diameter and supported by eight pillars, and, with the height of the Chattri itself being 29ft. and its position being 500ft. up on the Downs, the monument can be seen from miles away.

The Chattri was unveiled and dedicated by the Prince of Wales on 1st February, 1921, in the presence of the High Commissioner for India, Sir William Meyer, and members of the Council of the Secretary of State for India. A 21-gun salute honoured the Indian soldiers who had died in the war, and after the dedication a firing party of Royal Irish Fusiliers fired three volleys, each followed by a roll of drums.

The proposed inscription, which was not on the Chattri at the time of the unveiling, was

TO THE MEMORY OF ALL THE INDIAN SOLDIERS WHO GAVE THEIR LIVES IN THE SERVICE OF THEIR KING-EMPEROR IN THE GREAT WAR, THIS MONUMENT ERECTED ON THE SITE OF THE FUNERAL PYRE WHERE THE HINDUS AND SIKHS WHO DIED IN HOSPITAL IN BRIGHTON PASSED THROUGH THE FLAME, IS IN GRATEFUL ADMIRATION AND BROTHERLY AFFECTION DEDICATED.

The Scottish-American war memorial in Princes Street Gardens, Edinburgh, is a tribute to Scotland's effort in the Great War from men of Scottish blood and sympathies in America.

Entitled "The Call," it was unveiled by the American Ambassador, A. B. Houghton, on 7th September, 1927.

The sculptor was R. Tait Mackenzie of Philadephia, the architect was Reginald Fairley of Edinburgh, and the cost of the memorial was £10,000.

The sculptor had already completed war memorial commissions in North America and in Cambridge, where his bronze "The Home-Coming" formed the Cambridgeshire memorial.

His bronze figure of a kilted Scottish soldier, seated but alert and with a rifle across his knees, is the main feature of the Princes Street memorial. On a stone plinth, the figure faces Edinburgh Castle while behind it is a 50ft. long wall with a bronze frieze and an inscription. The inscription is a quotation from a poem by Lieutenant E. A. McIntosh, M.C. of the Seaforth Highlanders who was killed in 1916,

IF IT IS LIFE THAT WAITS I SHALL LIVE FOREVER UNCONQUERED,
IF DEATH, I SHALL DIE AT LAST, STRONG IN MY PRIDE AND FREE.

The frieze shows a procession of farm workers, shepherds and industrial workers, the

291   *The Belgian Monument, London*

292　　*The Scottish-American Memorial, Edinburgh*

figures changing half-way along into those of soldiers marching behind a pipe-band.

The heads of the men in the procession were said to have been modelled by the sculptor on those of men in the King's Own Scottish Borderers.

The Welsh National War Memorial stands in Alexandra Gardens, Cardiff. The idea of such a memorial was first mooted in 1917, but first started to take shape in October 1919 when the *Western Mail* opened a fund to which over £25,000 was soon subscribed.

Architectural assessors were appointed, designs were submitted by selected architects, and in July 1924 that of Mr. J. E. Comper was accepted. After some difficulty over choice of site it was decided in August 1925 that the memorial should be built in a central position in Alexandra Gardens, Cardiff. Messrs. E. Turner & Sons Ltd. were given the contract for the masonry work, Mr. W. D. Gough of Oxford was commissioned to execute the carving, Mr. A. B. Pegram to execute the sculpture, and Mr. A. B. Burton of Thames Ditton to cast the bronze.

Work commenced in March 1926 and was completed in the summer of 1928. The unveiling was on 12th June, 1928, by the Prince of Wales.

The memorial takes the form of a sunken court containing a central fountain and surrounded by a circular colonnade. As part of the fountain there are the bronze figures of a soldier, sailor and airman, each raising up a laurel wreath to a central and higher figure of a winged Messenger of Victory, his sword held aloft as if it were a cross. Beneath this figure is the inscription

IN HOC SIGNO VINCES (In this sign shalt thou conquer). On the frieze of the colonnade inside are carved the words of Sir Henry Newbolt,

293　　*The Welsh National War Memorial*

159

294   *The Welsh National War Memorial*

REMEMBER HERE IN PEACE THOSE WHO IN TUMULT OF
WAR BY SEA, ON LAND, IN AIR, FOR US AND FOR THE
VICTORY ENDURETH UNTO DEATH.

The inscription on the outside frieze reads,
I FEIBION CYMRU A RODDES EU BYWYD DROS EI
GWLAD YN RHYFEL MCMXIV-MCMXVIII.

(To the sons of Wales who gave their lives for
their country in the war of 1914-1918.)

Finally, there are appropriate inscriptions in
Welsh by poets William Parry and T. Gwyn Jones
over the three porches which lead to the figures
of the Soldier, Sailor and Airman. For example,
that above the sailor is DROS FOR FE DROES I FARW
(Over the sea went he to die).

In addition to this monument the names of
the Welsh men and women who fell in the war
were recorded by Mr. Graely Hewitt, a noted
artist in writing and illumination, in a
handsomely bound vellum book deposited in the
National Museum and later removed to the
Temple of Peace.

Today the monument stands in the middle of
beautifully-kept gardens and is a most impressive
and appropriate memorial. It would be
unfortunate if the attractive surrounding trees
were allowed to obscure a perfect view of it, but
no doubt this problem will be overcome when
necessary.

The Northern Ireland War Memorial,
commemorating the dead of both World Wars, is
a building in Waring Street, Belfast. The Building
Fund was launched in 1947 from unique offices
consisting of three old tramcars in a blitzed area
in the city centre. The Corporation donated a
free site, the former buildings on which had,
again, been destroyed by enemy bombing, and
the Government made a grant of £1 for every £1
subscribed. The eventual cost of the building was
some £150,000.

The architect chosen, after a competition
open to any British architect, was Michael
Bowley, an ex-serviceman from Sevenoaks, and
on 28th October, 1963, the Queen Mother
opened the new four-storey War Memorial
Building with its colonnade of dark blue slate.

Immediately inside the building is a Hall of
Friendship to symbolize the friendship between
the people of Ulster and the forces of the United
States who passed through the province on their
way to France. Beyond that is the Memorial Hall
with two Books of Remembrance containing
approximately 22,000 names of those from
Northern Ireland who died in both wars. The
books rest within a glazed bronze casket
supported on a block of Ulster granite. Also
within the Hall is a stained glass window with the
badges of the various services and a mass of
crosses to mark the sacrifice of the thousands of
individuals who died.

295   *The Northern Ireland War Memorial*
(Photograph — Messrs. Anderson and McMeekin)

160

296 *The Scottish National War Memorial, Padres*

Elsewhere in the building are a lecture hall to seat 300, committee rooms, and the offices of the Royal British Legion and various other ex-servicemen's organizations.

The idea of a National War Memorial for Scotland was first suggested in 1917 and in due course a committee was appointed with the Prince of Wales as President and the Duke of Atholl as Chairman. Subscriptions were invited from Scots both at home and overseas, the first subscription received, apparently, being one of £500 from a prominent businessman, and the second being half-a-crown from an ex-tinker who served with the Black Watch.

The architect chosen was Sir Robert Lorimer, and wherever possible Scottish materials and artists were employed. The selected site was, most appropriately, the Castle Rock in Edinburgh, and the memorial building forms the north side of Crown Square, at the highest part of the Castle and facing the historic and ancient Banqueting Hall. The building incorporates the walls of the former barracks and the style of the detail is characteristic of 16th century Scottish architecture (see Plate C29, p.114).

The memorial is basically rectangular in plan with projections into Crown Square at each end, and with a semi-circular projection on the opposite, or northern side. This apse faces the entrance porch and contains the shrine. Within the shrine the Castle Rock is exposed through the granite floor, and on it is the marble pedestal supporting the wrought steel casket which holds the Rolls of Honour with the names of the 100,000 Scottish dead of the Great War, to which were subsequently added those of the Second World War.

A bronze frieze round the walls of the shrine depicts a procession of Scots service-men and women in uniform, some 60 figures in all, and above there are seven stained-glass windows illustrating the Birth of War, the Overthrow of Tyranny, the Triumph of the Spirit, Praise, and Peace. Hanging from the vaulted roof, and directly above the casket, is an oak figure of St. Michael, a symbol of the triumph of Good over Evil (see Plate C30, p.114).

On either side of the entrance porch, and forming the bulk of the building, is the Hall of Honour with bays containing the memorials of the twelve Scottish Regiments, each with a stone

297 *The Scottish National War Memorial, Royal Engineers*

298   *The Scottish National War Memorial, Royal Artillery*

table on which rest Books of Remembrance. Also within the Hall are memorials to the various other arms and services, and further stained-glass windows, this time showing scenes of war. (see Plate C31, p.114).

The regimental memorials are to the Scots Guards, Royal Scots Greys, Royal Scots, Royal Scots Fusiliers, King's Own Scottish Borderers, Scottish Rifles (Cameronians), Black Watch, Highland Light Infantry, Seaforth Highlanders, Gordon Highlanders, Cameron Highlanders, and the Argyll and Sutherland Highlanders, and there are other memorials to the Royal Navy,

Flying Services, Royal Marines, Dominions and Colonies, Mercantile Marine, Scotswomen, Indian Army, Nursing Services, Padres, Royal Artillery, Household Cavalry, R.A.M.C., R.A.S.C., R.E., Scottish Yeomanry, Ordnance, Tank Corps, Veterinary Corps, Machine Gun Corps, London Scottish, South African Scottish, Liverpool Scottish, Tyneside Scottish, Canadian Scottish, and to Scots serving in English, Irish and Welsh Regiments.

There are coats of arms of counties and burghs; memorials to animals such as the one to "The Tunnellers' Friends" (canaries and mice),

299   *The Colour Parties (Photograph — Francis Caird Inglis)*

300   *The Official Party, with King George V, Queen Mary and the Prince of Wales (Photograph — Francis Caird Inglis).*

and one to carrier pigeons; beautiful stained glass; wonderful stone carvings and statues, both inside and on the exterior; and, in general, so many features and details that no short account can do the subject any justice at all. Of the books written about the memorial Ian Hay's *Their Name Liveth,* published shortly after the opening ceremony, is perhaps the best-known. The memorial is open to the public, and a visit is necessary for the scale, atmosphere and grandeur of the building to be fully appreciated.

About 200 artists and craftsmen contributed to the memorial and of these Alice Meredith-Williams modelled the figure of St. Michael in the shrine, Morris and Alice Meredith-Williams designed and modelled the bronze frieze in the shrine, Douglas Strachan was responsible for the stained-glass and Alex Carrick for the bronze panels to the Artillery and Engineers, and for the exterior figures of Justice and Courage.

The Prince of Wales formally opened the memorial on 14th July, 1927. Colour parties, to the music of *Scots Wha Hae* placed their colours within the building and then the Prince, in the uniform of the Royal Scots Fusiliers, of which he was Colonel-in-Chief, received the Rolls of Honour and placed them inside the casket. Each Roll was carried by an eminent personality, Field Marshal Earl Haig, for example, carrying the K.O.S.B. Roll, and while this ceremony took place the pipe lament *The Flowers of the Forest* was played.

The Rolls of the Royal Navy, Air Force and Scots Greys were held back to be placed in position by King George V, who arrived, with the Queen and Princess Mary, as the first visitor to the memorial, shortly after the opening ceremony by the Prince of Wales and the dedication by the Moderator of the General Assembly of the Church of Scotland, Dr. Norman Maclean.

As *The Scotsman* of the 15th July, 1927 put it, "Scotland, in the presence of the King and Queen, and through the lips of the heir to the throne, paid honour yesterday to her Glorious Dead."

The dead of the Great War have continued to be honoured for almost seventy years through the building, dedication and maintenance of such respected memorials, large and small, throughout the United Kingdom. It is to be hoped that such respect continues, and is extended to afford protection to other memorials which may seem, today, to be more at risk.

301   *The Scottish National War Memorial*

Acknowledgements

I should like particularly to thank my wife Rena for all her interest in, and assistance with this book, especially at the proof-reading stages, and also Barbara Jones for all her help with correspondence and, above all, for typing the manuscript, which by most standards might have been considered illegible.

I wish to acknowledge the following sources of information and to thank all those who took the time and trouble to provide background material. In particular, library services throughout the country have been most helpful and efficient.

Aberdeen Central Library
Aldershot Library
Mrs. J. Anderson
Mrs. M. Anderson
R. Anderson
Miss S. P. Andrews
Aylesbury County Library
Mr. J. Bagshaw
Margaret Baker — "Discovering London's Statues and Monuments"
Bank of England
Mr. D. R. Banting
Mr. T. C. Barker, Curator, Scottish National War Memorial
Mr. S. Barron
Mr. E. D. Bates
Bath Reference Library
Battersea District Library
Mrs. E. Baxter
Bedford Central Library
Bedfordshire Conservation Officer
Belfast City Hall
Belfast Linen Hall Library
Belfast Public Library
Mr. C. R. Betts
Mrs. D. Billingham
Mrs. I. Birch
Birkenhead Park Football Club
Birmingham Reference Library
Blackpool Gazette and Herald
Mrs. M. Blythe
Mr. G. Boddy
Bolton Evening News
Bournemouth County Library
Mr. L. J. Bowley
Mr. J. Boyd

Mrs. A. Boyle
P. J. Bracey
Bradford Central Library
Bradford Telegraph and Argus
Mrs. A. Brian
Hazel Brenchley
Mrs. M. Brightmore
Brighton Central Reference Library
Bristol Central Library
Mr. J. W. Brown
Miss M. B. Brown
Mrs. P. Brown
Mrs. V. Brown
Mrs. Y. Brown
Mrs. K. Buchanan
Mr. & Mrs. J. Buckley
Mrs. L. Burke
Mr. T. Burns
Mr. R. Butcher
Mrs. H. Caldwell
Betty Cambers
Cambridge Central Library
Camden Local History Library
Mr. J. G. Campbell
Cardiff Central Library
Mr. R. Cawood
Chelsea Library
Mrs. E. Chisholm
Mrs. J. G. Clark
Colchester Central Library
Mrs. W. A. Cooper
Mr. W. G. Corlett
Coventry Evening Telegraph
Mrs. A. M. Cracknell
Cumbria Record Office, Carlisle
Darlington County Library
Mrs. J. Darwent
Miss J. M. Deacon
Derby Central Library
Mr. I. Dewhirst
Dorset County Library, Dorchester
Mr. G. Dowler
Dumfries Ewart Library
Dundee Central Library
Durham County Library
Ealing Local History Library
Edinburgh Central Public Library
Mr. R. G. Edwards
Mr. R. Ellis
Mrs. D. Evans

Ewell Library
Exeter County Library
Mrs. E. P. Fletcher
T. Bailey Forman Ltd.
Mrs. I. M. Foulsham
Mr. F. A. Fowler
Mr. A. Fremlin-Bailey
H. Fretwell
Mr. H. Frost
Mrs. J. Furnivall
M. Gammon
Mr. E. S. Garbutt
Miss J. G. Garrow
Mr. M. Garrs
Mr. E. Gettens
Mr. R. Gibson
Mr. S. F. Girling
Glasgow Mitchell Library
Gloucester County Library
Anne Gordon
Mr. E. Green
Greenock Local History Library
Mrs. S. M. Grimshaw
Guildhall Library
Guildford County Library
Halifax Evening Courier
Miss M. Hall
Hammersmith and Fulham Libraries
F. Hards
Mrs. L. G. Hardy
Mrs. E. Harland
Mr. J. R. Harrison
Harrogate Library
Mr. Haste
Miss M. Haworth
Mrs. Hay
Muriel Herbert
Hereford City Library
Herts. Advertiser
Mrs. J. Hiddleston
Mr. R. J. Higgins
High Wycombe Central Library
Mr. E. W. Himsworth
Mr. A. Holmes
Rev. G. H. Holmes
House of Commons Public Information Office
Mr. G. B. Howcroft
Mr. J. B. Howcroft
Huddersfield Daily Examiner
Mrs. A. Hudson
Hull Central Library
Mr. D. Hullah
Mr. C. H. Hunt
Mr. R. Hunter
Huntingdon County Library
Mrs. B. Hutchinson
Imperial War Museum
Islington Central Library
Mrs. M. E. Jacques
Mr. F. G. Jeavans
Mrs. A. Johnson
Mr. G. Johnson
Mr. G. G. Jones
Mr. H. E. Jones
Mrs. M. S. Jones
Keighley Public Library
Mr. R. Kellie

Mr. C. Kennedy
Mrs. O. Kennedy
Kensington Central Library
Mrs. M. Kilgour
Mrs. E. Kilpatrick
Knaresborough Town Council
Mr. E. Ladds
Mr. W. J. Lea
Mr. L. Lean
Leeds Central Library
Leeds City Council
Leicester Library
Leicester Mercury
Mr. J. Lemmings
Mrs. M. Lewis
Lewisham Local History Centre
Lincoln Central Reference Library
Liverpool Daily Post and Echo
K. G. Locke
Londonderry Public Library
Mrs. S. MacIntyre
Mr. G. S. MacLachlan
Mr. D. J. MacLeod
Mr. A. J. Malcolm
Manchester Central Library
Mr. M. C. Mann
Mr. J. S. Marshall
Mr. S. A. Martin
Marylebone Library
Mrs. E. M. Mason
Group Captain H. S. Maurice-Jones
Mrs. V. A. Minter
Mrs. I. Mitson
Mrs. K. A. Moore
Mrs. E. Moralee
Mrs. E. A. Morgans
Wendy Morray-Jones
Mr. C. Mountain
Mr. J. Munro
Miss E. Munson
Mr. J. Murphy
National Maritime Museum
National Trust, Sandham Memorial
Newcastle Central Library
Newport Central Library
Mrs. O. M. Nicolle
Mrs. R. Norris
Northampton Central Library
Northern Echo
Norwich Central Library
Norwich Tourist Information Centre
Nottingham County Library
Mr. G. Odell
Oxford Central Library
Mr. R. Park
Mr. F. Parsons
Mrs. A. Passmore
Mr. J. Paterson
Mr. E. Peacock
Mr. & Mrs. J. Pearce
Peterborough Standard
Mrs. E. J. Phillips
Mrs. J. Phillips
Plymouth County Library
Mrs. J. E. Poole
Portsmouth Central Library
Reading Central Library

Redruth Library
Mary Repper
Richmond Reference Library
Mrs. E. Roscorla
Royal British Legion, Belfast
Rugby Library
Russell–Cotes Museum
St. Albans Central Library
Mrs. A. M. Scott
Shakespeare Birthplace Trust
Miss E. C. Shallard
Mrs. M. Shearing
Sheffield Central Library
Shrewsbury County Library
Mr. G. Shrubsole
Mr. C. Simpson
Mr. J. Slater
Mr. J. Smith
Mrs. K. Smith
Mrs. N. P. Smith
Dr. L. S. Snell
Mr. A. L. Soilleux
Southampton Central Library
Southern Evening Echo
South Wales Evening Post
Southwark Local Studies Library
Mr. R. Stannard
Mrs. G. Stewart
Mr. J. Stewart
Stockport Central Library
Stoke-on-Trent City Central Library
Mr. R. Stuart
Suffolk County Archivist
Surrey Comet
Swansea County Library
Mr. J. W. Syer
Mrs. J. S. Symon
Mr. A. C. Tallis
J. W. Tarrant

Mr. I. Taylor
Mr. J. Taylor
Mr. J. Theobald
Mr. J. Thomas, Newport Borough Council
Mr. R. Thomas
Mr. E. P. Thorne
Times Newspapers Ltd.
Mrs. K. Timms
Mrs. E. C. Titmarsh
Mrs. M. S. Toone
Trustees, Scottish National War Memorial
Twickenham Reference Library
Tyne and Wear Museums Service
Mr. A. Underwood
Valentines of Dundee Ltd.
Mr. J. Walcot
Mr. R. Walker
Mr. R. S. Ward
Mrs. E. Watkins
Wessex Newspapers
Mrs. E. Whild
Mr. L. White
Mr. S. E. Whitlock
Arnold Whittick — "War Memorials"
G. Wicks
Wiltshire Newspapers
Mrs. A. Winter
Wolverhampton Central Library
Woodbridge Museum
Mr. J. Woolley
Worcester County Records Office
Mrs. L. Yates
York Library

Finally, I should like to thank the many newspapers who kindly published appeals for information on my behalf.

Index

Bold figures indicate references to photographs

168

169